One Courageous Woman!,

Once I started reading this book, I couldn't put it down. This is a truly amazing story about the life of Iris...Her resilience is mind-boggling and one can only stand back in awe....I found it extremely inspirational.

Leila Summers- Author of It Rains In February

This is an important book, a book many readers won't be able to put down.... this book shows the immense resilience a human being, in this case Iris, can master in the face of almost insurmountable adversity. This book gives hope to people who are struggling with bad relationships, illness and other kinds of hardship. I like the style in which the book was written. You can hear Iris talking - telling you her story. She is a remarkable woman, who despite all she went through never lost her subtle sense of humour.

Fred Shaefer- Author of How To Make Great Things Happen In YOUR LIFE

NOT AGAIN

"My body's a write off but I'm all right."

Iris Ann Cullimore
(Narrator)

Richard von Hippel
(Author)

Peter Makem
(Editor)

*To all those organisations and individuals striving to
end all forms of domestic violence against all women
and to their raising of the awareness of the true extent
of domestic violence against disabled women*

ACKNOWLEDGEMENTS

My very special thanks go out to all of the following wonderful people, in the order I was lucky enough to meet them:

The young Casualty doctor who diagnosed me at the BRI
Dr Shaw who got me accepted at Pinderfields
Mr Towns (Neurological Consultant and Surgeon)
Mr Towns Secretary, Ann
The ITU Doctors and Nurses at Pinderfields
The ITU Doctors and Nurses at Bradford Royal Infirmary (BRI)
Eileen my Named Nurse (BRI)
Dr 'J' (Jay) Wright and his Staff Nurse, Sian (BRI)
The Ward 5 Nurses (BRI)
The BRI Physiotherapists
The St Lukes Physiotherapists
Mr Bollen (Orthpaedic Consultant and Surgeon)
Mr Bollen's Secretary, Maria
Doctor Corbridge (G.P.) my family doctor
Mr Wilkinson (Vascular Consultant and Surgeon)
Dr Reynolds (Gastroenterology Consultant)
Mr Griffith (General Surgeon/Colorectal Surgery Specialist)
Mr Griffith Secretary, Sharron
Mr Flannagan (Urological Consultant and Surgeon)
Mr Veysi (Orthopaedic Consultant and Surgeon)
Mr Veysi's Secretary, Jenny

And all the paramedics, casualty staff, radiographers, anaesthetists, doctors, nurses, healthcare assistants, physiotherapists, porters, and all of the people that keep a hospital going, like clerks, hospital cooks and cleaners; all of whom played a part in looking after me.

All images courtesy: http//www.dreamstime.com

INTRODUCTION

I was born into a better off than average family in 1951 at St Lukes Hospital, Bradford, West Yorkshire. My parents named me Iris Ann Stewart and I had a much better than average childhood until I was gang-raped when I was only eleven years of age.

From that day on my life kept being blown apart by so many life-shattering events that by the time I met my therapist in 2005, I'd survived being stalked by my violent ex-fiancé, a teenage pregnancy, being disowned by my dad, forced into marrying a violent, alcoholic, gambling addict, the premature death of my mother from a burst aneurysm (brain haemorrhage), yet another violently abusive marriage to a man who was later imprisoned for tying up a prostitute with wire before raping her at knifepoint, long term disability from my own burst aneurysm, multiple strokes, seizures, a tumour on the bowel and if it hadn't been for the brilliant doctors and surgeons who helped me I would have lost my left foot, my left leg and my life.

Now I do have to say that although I had to learn different ways to live and suffered no end of horrible health problems, I do not regret having been badly disabled by a brain haemorrhage (burst aneurysm) and multiple strokes, because not only did I get to meet so many wonderful people through them, but they also forced the real Iris to come out from where she'd been abused and bullied into hiding.

She is the Iris that wasn't afraid to stand her ground and fight her corner against bigger and rougher raised kids from a tough Estate and when she did come back she came out fighting for my survival. She's also stayed on to keep me so much stronger than I was before the aneurysm and I know that with her help and the good friends I've made along the way I'm going to have a lot more fun and lot more laughs in my life.

NOT AGAIN

"My body's a write off but I'm all right"

Chapter One

My parents had a lot in common when they met for the first time. Both of their families had deep Celtic and Roman Catholic roots. Dad's family were strict Scottish Catholics who'd moved to Bradford long before dad was born. Mum's family were strict Irish Catholics who'd moved to Bradford long before mum was born. Both were very young when one of their own parents died. Both of their families had their own business on Bowling Back Lane. Mum and dad were already working most of their free time in their own family's business before they met at school.

Mum was only a baby when her father abandoned her and her mother to make a new life for himself in Australia. Then mum's mother died of a brain haemorrhage (burst aneurysm) when mum was only eleven years old. Her father did come back from Australia to take her to live with him, but mum couldn't forgive him for deserting her and her mother, so she wouldn't go with him and in the end her dad had to go back to Australia on his own, leaving mum with her three aunties to look out for her.

Two of her aunties were her mother's sisters, the other auntie was married to her mum's brother and they all treated her like a workhorse at home and in the Café they owned on Bowling Back Lane. But they weren't being cruel to her because even though they made her work hard her aunties always made sure mum never wanted for anything through all the time she was growing up with them.

Dad's father never recovered his health after being gassed in the First World War and he died when dad was only about eight or nine. But dad was a little bit luckier than mum because he had his mother and his father's two brothers to look out for him. Not that he got his uncles' help for nothing because even though dad should have inherited his father's share of the business he had to earn his keep by spending most of his spare time working for his father's brothers in J Shaw and Sons Bradford Waste, a big waste paper trading business his grandfather built up on Bowling Back Lane.

That's just the way it was in those days. There'd been a world war and a depression. People died young all of the time. There was no time for sympathy and you just got on with it the best way you could. You got nothing for free from anyone and families were expected to help each other out. If you were big enough to earn your keep you earned it without feeling sorry for yourself and that's what mum and dad were doing when he saw her for the first time at St Peter's Roman Catholic School, off Leeds Road, Bradford, West Yorkshire.

The boys' playground and the girls' playground at St Peter's were kept separate by a low wall but the boys' playground overlooked the girls' playground and one day dad saw mum doing handstands at playtime. The next day when dad saw mum walking to school he started teasing her about her navy blue knickers and mum must have liked the teasing because after that they started walking each other to school and back.

Before long they were boyfriend and girlfriend without needing to ask each other. Neither of them ever went out with anyone else and they got married when dad was eighteen and mum was twenty-one. The reason they got married when they did was because dad got called up for the war and I think mum got pregnant with their first child while they were on their Honeymoon.

When Dad went into the army he started out as a lorry driver and I don't know how long it was before he became a despatch rider. The main thing is that he managed to get through the war safely and when he got home dad went straight back to working for his father's two brothers at Bradford Waste. There he worked his way up to being in charge of the firm's fleet of lorries, along with their two waste paper storage and sorting warehouses in Bradford.

One of Bradford Waste's warehouses was round Payley Road, near Bowling Park and the other warehouse was at Bowling Back Lane. Dad had two managers working under him but he didn't really like the managing side of the business. What he really loved was long-distance driving, and having two managers in the office gave him a lot more time to spend on the road. But the biggest reason why dad managed to do so much long-distance driving was because he built up such a good relationship with the Gypsies who traded with Bradford Waste.

Dad always treated the Gypsies fairly with the prices he paid them for their waste paper and he always freely gave them the really good new clothes the catalogue people were forever leaving in the returns boxes. He always put money behind the bar in their local pub for them, and in return they kept an eye on Bradford Waste for dad and made sure that no one ever broke in or stole from it.

While dad was away at the war, mum's three aunties carried on treating her like a workhorse and even though mum had her own job working on pistons at the engineering firm of Hepworth and Grandage, she was still expected to go down to the Café and help out in the mornings before she went to work, as well as during the lunch break at her own job. Her aunties didn't give her any lunchtime at the café, either. If mum wanted lunch she had to make it for herself and eat it on the way to the café and back to work, or when she was delivering meals to the elderly and disabled in the evenings after her work, because everyone had to help out in the war and that was her job for the Café.

It must have been twelve to thirteen years after the war was over and mum was still grafting for the Café when I was big enough to peel a potato and prepare a vegetable. Then I was expected to go with mum to the Café, where I had to help out with peeling their big sacks of 'taties' (potatoes), especially when the machines broke down. This happened a lot and you couldn't finish until all the work was done. That's how I found out how hard they'd been making mum work ever since her mother died.

One way or another, both my parents had never stopped grafting for their families or their country when they'd made their first home on Stamford Street. Life didn't get any easier for them as their first baby died at birth. The baby would have been my older sister if she'd lived, but mum said she never stood a chance. The pregnancy had been so hard on mum and the delivery was so dangerous for both mum and the baby that they had to choose between them, and they chose mum over the baby.

Mum nearly lost her next baby through high blood pressure and they made her stay at home for most of the pregnancy just as she had to do with me, but she managed to keep the baby and gave birth to a healthy boy. That was three years before she gave birth to me in St Lukes Hospital, Bradford on the 13th of October 1951.

I had such a serious breathing problem when I was born that no one expected me to live. Someone had to stay with me night and day for the first few weeks of my life just in case I stopped breathing and died, but whatever the doctors did for me something came right with my breathing and I had no more problems with it until I was over four years old.

Up until then I was having a really good life growing up at Stamford Street with mum and dad. They were very, very close with each other and I was very, very close to both of them. Nearly every night mum would sit in her chair and I would sit on the floor while she brushed and stroked my hair for ages. When mum wasn't brushing and stroking my hair I would be playing with my doll or sitting on dad's lap, getting a cuddle and playing games.

Every Thursday dad would buy mum a big box of Black Magic chocolates and bring her flowers. We always got loads of sweets as well and I always looked forward to Thursdays. We never went without anything we really needed, and there was always at least one car in the drive that dad would use for taking us all away for weekend trips whenever he could. We mostly went driving round the East Coast where we had a caravan at Flamborough Head, and every year we went to see the Illuminations in Blackpool with my Uncle Bill and my Aunt Connie Iris. They were on my dad's mother's side of the family and they named me Iris after her.

They were good days for me and life would have been perfect if it wasn't for my older brother, who was the only odd-one-out in the family. Most of the time he kept himself to himself, reading or doing whatever it was that he did on his own in his own room. The only times he ever seemed to come out of his room and join in with the family - apart from weekend trips - was when he wanted to eat or to torment me. Like the time I was washing my doll's clothes in the sink and I left her alone while I went off to the toilet. While I was gone my brother put my doll in the sink and poured boiling water all over her. When I came back from the toilet I found my doll all melted up in the sink. I was heartbroken.

I don't know if he was trying to spite me for taking over from him as the 'baby' of the family, or if he was just 'that way out' as we say in Yorkshire. Whatever the reason, he was the one that always lost out. Keeping himself to himself most of the time gave me loads more time to do things alone with mum or dad and there was a lot for me to do with them. Mum was a really good swimmer and she started teaching me to swim every week. I was so young that I don't even remember the first time she ever took me to a swimming pool.

Dad's great uncle bred horses on a farm he owned over at Denholme and they started teaching me to ride horses there from when I was really small. That's how I got my lifelong love of swimming and horses, and out of the two it was always the horses I loved the most. Just being around horses makes me feel good but riding a horse makes me feel really free and I would have liked to have gone horse riding and swimming all day, every day, if it wasn't for my parents working and for me having to go to St Columba's Nursery School, off Leeds Road, where I walked out the gates at lunchtime, on my very first day.

Dad caught me trying to walk my own way back home and he'd taken me straight back to nursery school where they all gave me a big warning against wandering off again. But they needn't have bothered, because it took me no time at all to get on really well with all the other kids, and after that first day I spent most of my time playing and having nothing but fun. That is until the day I was brought home early from nursery to find mum being put into an ambulance.

Mum had miscarried the baby that should have been my older sister and I know I was only about four years old at the time but I'll never forget seeing the midwife with the perfectly formed, perfectly still little body that should have been my younger brother, and I can still see dad having to clean up on his own after mum and the midwife had left. As far as I remember there was no talk of the miscarriage when mum came back from the hospital but they both wasted no time in finding us a new home on Gledhill Road, off Leeds Road.

Chapter Two

We were right in the middle of moving into our new home on Gledhill Road when my breathing suddenly started to go wrong again and mum got so worried that she rushed me to our new doctor's surgery. There the new doctor told her I only had about two weeks to live and he sent for an ambulance to take me to hospital but dad turned up before the ambulance arrived and he rushed me off to see Dr Edwards, who'd been our doctor when we lived on Stamford Street.

By the time we got to Dr Edwards surgery I had to fight for every breath but the receptionist wouldn't let us in. All she kept saying, over and over again was that Dr Edwards wasn't our doctor any more and that they weren't letting anyone else in.

Mum really trusted Dr Edwards and no one was going to stop her from getting me in to see him. So she just waited outside until they were letting someone out of the surgery and then she sneaked us in but the

Receptionist spotted this and there was another and even bigger argument.

When Dr Edwards heard all the commotion he came out to see what was happening and mum showed me to Dr Edwards who got so angry with the Receptionist that he was shouting at her. "What's the matter with you! Can't you see! Look at her! She's nearly blue! Get an ambulance! Now!"

Once again my parents didn't wait for an ambulance to take me to hospital. They ran to the car and dad drove us to the Children's Hospital at Lister Park, where both of them made such a fuss about me that a doctor came and saw me straight away.

I think he was only trying to calm them down at first but when he took a proper look he told my parents I was going to have to stop over in the hospital, which scared me so much they had to drag me fighting and crying all the way to the Ward. I was fighting that hard I don't know how the nurses managed to hold onto me let alone undress me and put me into a bed.

I got even more scared when I heard them telling my parents that they couldn't stop in there with me. I'd never been left on my own in my life and I fought so hard they were forced to hold me down in the bed. But it was no good trying to fight them off because in those days hospitals were really strict, much stricter than they are with children today and it made no difference to them that I was fighting and crying my head off.

Now it's too long ago and I was too upset to remember how long it took me to realise that I could fight and cry all I wanted but I was going to stay on that

Ward whether I liked it or not. What I do remember is that when it did sink in, I settled down and that's when I really noticed there were six other children on the Ward. Some of them were too poorly to talk at all but there was one little boy, right opposite me, who could talk and we took to each other straight away.

We became such good friends that I was always in his bed, or he was in mine and the funny thing is, being as strict as it was, Matron and none of the nurses minded the two of us being in and out of each others beds all the time. In fact they even took a picture of Matron and the nurses standing round my bed with the two of us in it together.

Making friends with that little boy helped me settle down and with mum and dad coming to see me every day I knew they weren't going to leave me there on my own, which made me feel a lot safer. Then after a little while Matron gave me the job of sharing out the Ward sweets every day, which I really enjoyed. But sharing out sweets and feeling safer never stopped me from being frightened to death when they told me I had to have an operation, which I didn't understand at all.

I'm sure the doctors must have told mum and dad what my operation was all about but no one explained any of it to me. I suppose they didn't bother to do that with children in those days. All I was told was that it had something to do with my breathing, and someone said something about a valve.

I didn't know what a valve was, so I didn't fret until they told me I was going to have the operation the next day and then I got really frightened again, but a very nice doctor must have known how frightened I was and when it was time to go for the operation he came onto the Ward, put me up on his shoulders and carried me all the way to the operating theatre, telling me jokes and trying to make me laugh along the way.

That's all I really remember until I woke up feeling horrible, but feeling horrible was nothing to the pain I got from the three injections they gave me every single day and it wasn't long before my backside got that sore from all those injections they had to hold me down every time they came to give me another one.

I fought so hard against those injections the doctors ended up making me stay in hospital for about six weeks until I didn't need them any more and they let me go home. I was so happy to see the back of that hospital I never wanted to go into another one, ever again. But I didn't get my wish because it was only a couple of months before I was back again, only this time I was luckier than the last time.

All they did was take my tonsils out and then I was back at our new home, eating loads of ice cream and getting to know all about our new life around Gledhill Road where there was a big field and a wood on the one side of us but there was a rough estate only a couple of streets away.

That rough estate was full of big families of hard men and hard women. Their kids were used to seeing arguments being settled with fists and they were as hard as their parents. Fighting was just a way of life on that estate and later on I found out there were proper bare-knuckle fights for money going on all the time, but

I didn't know any of that when I first met up with some of the estate kids who came down to play on the field and in the woods.

I wasn't allowed to play in the woods because my parents couldn't keep an eye on me there, but I was allowed to play on the field where they could see me from the house, and that field is where I learned how to stand up to rougher and harder kids than my old friends on Stamford Street.

These new kids didn't settle their differences with shouting and arguing like the kids at Stamford Street. If this lot didn't like what you did or said you were in for a fight, and that went for the lasses as well as the lads.

More lads than lasses came down to the field but you had to stand up to both if you wanted to get on, and my parents made sure I got on. There was no running home crying from being picked on. If I went whining to mum and dad then one or both of them would give me a 'crack' and send me back out to finish my side of the argument.

My parents weren't being cruel or being hard on me. They had to do the same when they were growing up and they knew it would have been worse for me if they'd interfered. So I learned how to stand up for myself.

Sometimes I won and sometimes I lost but I always stood my ground. That way the other kids respected me and I respected them, which led to us all having a lot of fun playing together on that field and on the street outside our house.

But my brother was treated a lot different than me. He never got 'cracked' for not standing his ground, which is probably why he never stood up for himself and that made him show me up so bad.

When we were kids he was always running away from one set of lads or another and they picked on him all the more for it, which nearly always ended up with him hurting himself more with the running away than he would have done if he'd stood his ground.

There was the time he was running away from one set of lads when he tripped and fell on a tin can, with the lid still attached and the lid sliced his leg so bad you could see the bone. Another time when he was running away from a different set of lads my brother tripped and fell on the railway tracks, knocking his shoulder right out.

Running away is why my brother was always covered in cuts and bruises from falling over. That's why he was forever in casualty at the BRI (Bradford Royal Infirmary). And in the end he got so well known for his running away that everyone used to say that I should have been the boy and he should have been the girl.

You would have thought that with all of his running away and making a fool of himself my brother would have stopped from trying to torment me but nothing seemed to be able to stop him until I started standing up to him as well.

As soon as I started standing up to him he took to spending more and more time alone in his room and I started spending more and more time playing with the other kids, when I wasn't going to nursery, or going on long-distance driving with my dad in the firm's lorries, or going horse riding at dad's great uncle's farm, or going swimming with my mum.

Mum had made sure I was a really good swimmer by the time we moved to Gledhill Road, where she thought it was time for me to join a proper swimming club. So she took me down to Feversham Street Swimming Baths and put me into the Nignogs Swimming Club, which is such a funny name that a black friend of mine burst out laughing and couldn't stop smiling when I recently told him that I used to be a Nignog.

My friend asked me if they called them Nignogs because there were a lot of black people in the club and I told them it couldn't have been that. There were loads of Nignogs swimming clubs all over the country and they'd been there long before black people really started coming to England when the war was over.

Our club alone must have taught thousands of kids to swim until it closed in the 1970's, so it couldn't have been anything to do with colour, but my friend was still so curious about the name they looked it up for me and this is what they found out.

It seems like the name Nignogs was taken from a cartoon series about the 'hullo' Imp Twins, Nig and Nog, who lived on the moon and they had loads of cartoon adventures ('nig' and 'nog' were also said to be County Durham slang words for 'boy' and 'girl', which fitted just as well, because the Nignogs were swimming clubs for boys and girls).

15

Our local newspaper, the Telegraph and Argus, sponsored the Bradford Nignogs swimming club. We all got a little blue enamel badge with a funny little face in gold on it and a lot of us were lucky enough to get our names in the newspaper when it was our birthday.

It's a long time ago since I joined the Nignogs but I still have lots of good memories of competing and winning against other Nignogs, even though I was only about seven years old when I started with the competitions. When I was old enough I joined the 'Nignog Floaters' formation swimming team, which took me to loads of different places, competing in the swimming and giving formation demonstrations.

Swimming is something I still love and I'm trying to get started again but my biggest love of all is still horses. There was a time when I wanted a horse of my own but my dad wouldn't let me have one. He said I had nowhere close to home to look after it and I wouldn't have time when I went to proper school. That hurt me a lot when he said it, but I was that busy doing other things I didn't have much time to be sad.

Anyway, there were always the horses on the farm for me to ride whenever I managed to pester dad into taking me over to Denholme, where I did have a favourite horse I could ride any time I wanted- as long as the 'mucking out' and the rest of the stable work was done.

I know it's been a long time since then but I've never lost that childhood love of horses. I even managed to go riding over at Shelf Moor as soon as I recovered enough from my brain haemorrhage and the first lot of strokes. I would still like to go horse riding, even after all the trouble they had giving me a new hip after my first operation went so badly wrong and nearly left me with no hip at all.

But strokes and broken hips were a long way off from then, and in the meantime I had to start working in the Café as well as starting to earn my own pocket money. Mum and dad said I had to learn the value of money, same as they had to do when they were growing up, so they gave me jobs to do round the house. The jobs got bigger as I got bigger and got more pocket money, but I didn't mind. I liked learning to make my own clothes and do cooking and I liked helping mum to keep a nice home.

The only thing that really annoyed me about having to earn my own pocket money was mum and dad giving my brother his pocket money, without him having to earn it. I think that was because they couldn't stand him whining every time he was asked to do something, which was something I never did.

Whatever work I was given I just got on with it and I was earning my own pocket money every week by the time I was sent to St Peters Catholic School, where mum and dad had met for the very first time.

Chapter Three

I was about five years old when I was taken out of St Columba's nursery school and sent to St Peter's Roman Catholic School, where some of the teachers were 'ordinary' people but mostly nuns.

All of the nuns were good to all of us and we liked them all. I always had the same teacher, Sister Gemma. I was teacher's pet, and my 'special' friend at St Peter's was a girl I'm going to call Mary.

We 'connected' from the moment we met and we stayed best friends all the way through our time at St Peter's but I'm not going to say what Mary's real name was because her childhood was so hard it wouldn't be fair on her. If Mary wants anyone else to know what her real name was, then she can tell it herself.

What I will say about Mary is that we were always together at school and we would help each other out, even when we didn't really need any help. That was most of the time because nearly all of our lessons were easy and the only homework we ever got, aside from having to take home and read storybooks with pictures, was reading the Bible and learning our Catechism off by heart.

English was the only subject I never liked. I didn't like reading the picture books at home, so I made up the stories from looking at the pictures and mum thought I was right good at reading, which made her really proud of me. She never stopped telling me what a good reader I was. Little did she know I was making it all up!

Religion was different. I loved religion and that's where my Auntie Jessie really helped me out. She was religious mad and it was religion, religion, religion all of the time. Auntie Jessie knew that much about religion I didn't need anyone else to help me out with my Bible reading and learning my Catechism.

Auntie Jessie and her husband Uncle John were not my real aunties and uncles. Auntie Jessie had been mum's best friend from when they were at school together and they'd stayed best friends all of their lives. She was always there in the background and we were either at her house, or she was at ours.

It was Auntie Jessie who always wanted me to be a model when I grew up. She was the one who taught me to walk with books on my head and how to do all the things a model needed to do properly, like walking, turning and sitting. She always walked really straight and upright herself and I remember her always telling me- "Stand up straight. Tuck in your tummy. Chest out!"

I liked all that learning to be a model but I was still too young to think that much about being one, so it was mostly the horse riding, swimming and long-distance driving that was on my mind most of the time, until the religion took over and then I started spending as much time as I could with the nuns up there at the Convent.

That Convent was so nice inside and outside it was beautiful, especially their Grotto with Our Lady's statue in it and St Bernadette kneeling down. It was so beautiful and peaceful up there that I couldn't help myself from wanting to be around that Convent all the time and my parents didn't mind me going up there after school to help the nuns out with things like preparing meals and cleaning. I spent so much of my time there with the nuns that in the end I wanted to be one myself and my parents, being religious themselves, let me go for a two weeks 'experience' at another Convent, with a group of 15 to 20 girls I'd never met before.

We'd come from all over the country and all of us were really excited about learning to be nuns but the excitement soon wore off when we found out how horrible the food was and how little we got of it. We ate with the nuns and they got the same as us, which made me wonder how the fat nuns managed to get fat.

At the time I thought they must be eating loads of sweets on the sly, and there must have been plenty of sweets for them to eat because they'd searched our bags as soon as we arrived and anything nice we had to eat got taken off us, which was a shame, because learning to be a nun at that Convent was the most boring time I ever had in my life.

The most exciting things we ever did for two weeks were going to mass, praying, polishing, cleaning and meditating in our rooms. Worst of all were the days they wouldn't let us talk at all. I liked to talk and that really got me down. What with that and the boredom I soon gave up thinking about being a nun and joined the majorettes instead.

When I went back to school I told my best friend Mary all about it and she didn't think too much of my 'experience'. It never entered my head at the time and I never thought to ask her later, but maybe it was too close to her own life.

Mary lived in a children's home where she had a horrible time there and she never had much of anything.The rest of us had different clothes we could wear to school for a change but all Mary ever had to wear to school was a gingham dress.

Loads of kids at the school always used to pick on Mary and taunt her with things like, "You're from a home". "You don't have no mum and dad." and all this sort of thing. I used to stick up for her and tell them "Leave her alone, it's not her fault," and so on.

Mary never said it to me but I knew her worst day at school was our first day of going back after the Christmas holidays. I always felt right sorry for her then, because one of the first things we always had to do was write a story about what we did at Christmas and what we got for Christmas presents.

Everyone but Mary always spent loads of time writing down what they did and what they got, but she never had anything to write about. The Home she lived in never did anything much at Christmas and all she ever got was an apple, an orange and the one little something and nothing.

It wasn't much better the rest of the year for Mary. They were right strict with her all of the time and she couldn't even play out with the rest of us after school because she had to go straight back to the Home, have her tea and then do whatever it was they did in that Home. That place was so hard on her they wouldn't even let her go out on family trips with me and my parents at the weekends.

My parents did ask them for me but the Home just said no. So I was always asking mum and dad if she could come and live with us. I knew we could afford it but they always said "No! No! No!" and they just wouldn't have it. So when we were about 8 years old we made up our minds to run away.

At the time I was getting money to buy things every day at school and I was earning about half a crown (12 1/2 pence) a week from doing my pocket money jobs around the house. We used the money to buy running away from home food, like buttered teacakes and those little Hovis loaves.

Both of us saved up our school milk and we hid everything in our 'pump' (sports) bags, but one day Sister Gemma looked in our bags and found all the food and milk. Then she made us go into the cloakroom and eat the lot in one go. God it was awful! But that didn't stop us from running away!

Instead of going home after school one day we ran

off to a friend's house who said we could stop for a bit. It was exciting at first but then it started getting dark and the darker it got the more we panicked until we were panicking so much we decided to go home to my house.

When we got to our drive there was a police car parked outside so we hid behind some bushes until they went away. By the time they did go away we were so cold and frightened that we got up the nerve to go inside and as soon as mum and dad saw us they tore into the both of us. We got a right telling off from them and when they finally finished they called the police back again.

The police came back and gave us another right telling off, with things to me like "What do you think you're playing at! Can't you see the state your mum's in!" and they told Mary that the Home was really worried about her along with loads of stuff like that to both of us.

After the police finished they took Mary back to the Home, where she got another right telling off and as soon as the police had left with her, dad picked me up by the ankles and smacked me on the backside. Then they grounded me for a month and stopped all my money while I was grounded which meant I had to do all my jobs round the house for nothing and didn't get money for buying things at school.

Next day the nuns collared us again and they gave us another right lecture about running away. I can still hear them going on with things like "What on earth were you two thinking about! Anyone could have picked you up! Anything could have happened to you!" Then it was Sister Gemma's turn to collar us. She went on and on with more things like, "I knew the two of you were up to something. I should have known you were up to no good."

By that time we'd been told off so much it went right over our heads but I couldn't get used to being grounded with no money of my own. So I decided to get myself a paper round and earn my own money. The only paper round I could get that was close to home was on the rough estate near Gledhill Road and when I went for the job the paperman warned me it was a hard paper round. He said they'd lost loads of paperboys and girls through the way the kids behaved on the estate but I wasn't bothered, and that was a big mistake.

I didn't know anyone on the rough estate but the kids up there knew me by sight and they knew my family were well off. As soon as they saw me they ganged up and started taunting me about being a 'little rich girl' and loads of other things like that, but I wouldn't back down.

Next day the same thing happened and when I wouldn't back down they ran at me, swinging their fists and kicking out at me. They were all lads and they knew they could threaten me and try to scare me but they couldn't hit a girl. So the next day I turned up they'd brought some lasses down with them and they started on me.

The slapping and pushing I got from the lasses soon turned to kicking and punching and then they grabbed me by the hair. That got me so mad I fought them back but while I was fighting off the lasses some of the lads stole my paperbag. They threw all the papers away and then they ran off, still taunting me.

When I went back to the shop and told the man what had happened to his papers he said that he understood and I could stop doing the round if I wanted. But I wasn't going to let that lot stop me from earning my own money and I went back the next day.

I don't think the paperman expected me back again but he gave me the bag full of papers and I went off to the estate, where they were waiting for me. The lasses started kicking and punching me again and that went on for about a week until one day they were in the middle of kicking and punching me when the dad to one of the lads who was taunting me saw what they were doing.

The lad's father was one of the Gypsies who looked out for Bradford Waste for my dad and he gave all the kids a right 'clattering' for hitting me. He also told them all who my dad was and what he meant to the Gypsies. Then he warned them to leave me alone, which they did but not until after they'd given me a right thrashing for the 'clattering' they'd got.

After a while some of the same kids who'd started off with taunting and hitting me were coming down to the house to play so dad gave us a load of the rope they used for tying the wagons and there was soon a big gang of us kids, skipping and playing 'tin can squat' in the street outside the house and in the field next to us (See end of Chapter for 'tin can squat').

In between playing with the kids from the rough

estate I was going to school, working in the café, going long-distance driving with dad, doing formation swimming and competing with the NigNogs, practicing baton twirling for the majorettes, learning to cook and keep a home with mum, learning to knit, crochet, sew and make clothes to a proper dress pattern with Auntie Jessie, earning my pocket money with jobs round the house, and on top of all that I'd joined a proper dance class when I was about six years old.

I'd started off with learning to do ballet but that only lasted until some lasses told me they 'chopped your big toe off' to make your feet fit the 'blocks' in the toes of your ballet shoes, which put me right off and I gave up the ballet to learn Latin American dancing and Ballroom instead.

That's the busy way my life was going until I left St Peter's and went to St Blaise, when I was about eleven years old. As for my friend Mary, I didn't see her for years after we left St Peter's. Mary got sent to a different school and we didn't meet up again until after my brain haemorrhage, when they were trying to get me walking again with physiotherapy up where the old Casualty was at the BRI.

I was being wheeled out of one door and we were heading for another door when I heard this lass shouting "Hiya, Iris!" I looked back at her and I didn't recognise her at first but then the lass came up to me and said, "You haven't changed a bit."

I still didn't get who she was, but she carried on talking and the more she talked the more familiar she became until I suddenly realised it was my best friend

Mary from St Peter's. She'd gone on to do so well for herself. She was a Sister over one of the Departments at the BRI (Bradford Royal Infirmary) and she'd recognised me straight away after all that time!

Seeing how well Mary had got on after her bad start in the Children's Home made me so happy for her and we saw quite a lot of each other after our first meeting since we left school. There was a lot to talk about but the one part of my life I never shared with Mary was what happened to me in my first term at St Blaise'.

Note:
There were different ways to play 'tin can squat'. The way we played it started out with two teams and each team had from two kids upwards.

One team hid while the other team went looking for them and anyone they caught was 'OUT', unless one of their team mates managed to kick the can over and then they were 'FREE' again.

The team that was looking for those hiding had to defend the can and it wasn't their turn to hide until they'd caught all of the team that was hiding.

If there were many playing the game it could go on for hours before the team that was looking had a chance to hide, so they really defended the can. That could make it a very rough game, because there were no referees and arguments got sorted the usual way.

Chapter Four

The best thing about going to St Blaise was being told it was going to be nuns teaching us, just like St Peter's. But I soon found out the hard way that the nuns at St Blaise were nothing like the nuns at St Peter's. These new nuns were horrible and the worst of them all was the Deputy Head over the girls. Her name was Sister Immaculata and we used to call her evil, the way kids do when they really hate someone.

There are a lot of things I could say about my experiences of Sister Immaculata but I'm not going to. Not after my writing helper told me she died in 2008, which means she can't defend herself. So the only thing I am going to say about Sister Immaculata is that she made it her job to cane me every morning, with six of the best and her excuse was always the same, "Your fringe is too long. And so are your fingernails."

It wouldn't have been so bad if she'd been caning me for something I'd done because I could have taken her beatings if I'd deserved them but being beaten for nothing at all, every single morning, along with the beatings I was getting from the other nuns and teachers, without being able to fight back, finally got on top of me and I told my mum what was happening to me.

When mum heard about all the caning I was getting from Sister Immaculata she blew her top and mum was really angry when she said, "It's up to me to look after your hair and your nails! Her job is to teach you!"

Mum was only a tiny woman but the following morning she took me to St Blaise where she collared Sister Immaculata and gave her such a telling off that I was never beaten for my fringe or my fingernails, ever again.

That's all I'm going to say about the way I was treated by Sister Immaculata, because the person who told me she died also told me a lot of people had many good things to say about her. They said she'd set up vocational courses in hairdressing and nursing for girls way ahead of her time and that she'd also started a Halfway House for men with drug and alcohol addiction.

But I can only tell it the way it happened to me and, to be fair, she wasn't the only one that was quick to give you a beating for doing nothing wrong, or for something that wasn't your fault. She was just worse to me than the rest of the teachers who all had their favourite things to beat us with.

Our English teacher had a thick leather belt he would whack you with.

Our Maths teacher would hit you on the hands with a thick wooden block.

Our Music teacher used to throw the big wooden blackboard rubber at us and he wasn't bad with his aim.

Most of the beatings I got at St Blaise weren't even my fault, like the time we were supposed to play netball and all the balls were missing from our gym, so our gym teacher sent me over to the boy's gym to fetch them back and their gym teacher caught me in there.

"Oh! I've come for the netballs," I told him.

"You shouldn't be in here," he said to me.

"But I was sent here. The teacher sent me in here. Ask her," I replied.

Telling the truth made no difference to him and he gave me six of the best on my backside with a cricket bat, without even bothering to ask my gym teacher if I was telling the truth, and I can't even begin to tell you how bad six of the best with a cricket bat can hurt when the one that's doing the beating is a grown man and the one that's getting beaten with a cricket bat is just an eleven year old girl.

I suppose I was lucky we didn't have him for our sports lessons as well, which were bad enough without him. Up to then I'd always loved anything to do with sports but our sports lessons at St Peter's were very different to our sports lessons at St Blaise where the boys wore shorts and T-Shirts while we girls had to wear a T-Shirt and maroon coloured flannelette knickers, unless you were in a team and then you got to wear a maroon skirt over your knickers.

31

When I say knickers I don't mean those long things with elastic at the bottom of the legs. The knickers they forced us to wear for our sports lessons at St Blaise were more like those really skimpy things some women athletes wear today, which in those days would have been banned by anyone else.

Just doing our sports lessons in nothing but a T-Shirt and knickers was bad enough but we also had to wear them in public, when we were running down the road to the field where we started our cross-country runs. All of us girls hated running in public dressed like that with everyone watching and staring at us.

To this day I still do not know how a Roman Catholic school could have allowed us girls to be exposed like that, especially when the boys didn't have to go running and doing all their sports in their underpants. So it was lucky for me that I was really good at all sports and I was on a team so fast I was wearing a maroon skirt over my knickers before my first term was over.

Having a maroon skirt to wear over my knickers did make a big difference to my life at St Blaise, which would have been even better if it wasn't for the teachers. And I couldn't have been happier than I was when the time came for us to break up for our Summer Holidays. But I might not have been so happy if I'd known that one of my two new friends at St Blaise was going to get me into the worst kind of trouble.

My new friend's real name was Linda and we'd arranged for me to go over with her to Fagley, where she and our other friend lived. All we wanted to do was get together and play in the holidays and we were going to meet up with our other friend at their home, then the three of us were going to play in the fields at the side of her house.

My parents would have grounded me if they'd known I was going to stray so far from home and the way things turned out it would have been a lot better for me if they had grounded me on the day Linda came over to take me to Fagley on the bus, because our other friend wasn't at home when we got to her house and we went down to the fields to look for her.

When we got to the fields the only ones there were at the bottom of the hill and they were a gang of bikers. Well, that's what we called them in those days but the truth is that they were just a big gang of scruffy looking sixteen and seventeen year olds with only a couple of motorbikes between them.

One of the bikers was a lad we recognised from the senior year at St Blaise and Linda kept saying "Oh come on! Let's go down and see what they're doing."

I had more sense than that and I wasn't going down there with that lot so I told Linda I was going straight back home. But Linda wouldn't listen to sense and she started walking down the hill towards them while I started walking back the way we came.

I'd nearly reached the fence at the top of the field when I heard all this horrible yelling and screaming and when I looked round Linda was at the bottom of the field, pinned flat on the ground, with the gang trying to rip her clothes off.

Without stopping to think I ran down the hill and

right into the middle of them, where I fought with the gang until Linda got free but instead of staying and helping me Linda just ran away and left me on my own with the bikers who turned on me.

I fought like I never fought before. But it was no use. I was only eleven. They were sixteen and seventeen. There were too many of them for one small girl and they raped me.

Now I am not going to talk about the details, or how long it went on before they ran off, leaving me lying on the ground with no clothes on but when I got dressed, as best as I could, there wasn't a sign of Linda. I had to catch the bus and go home on my own, with my skirt ripped and no buttons left on my blouse and feeling like everyone was staring at me.

I tried to sneak into the house when I got home but mum caught me before I could get through the front door and she could have suspected what had happened to me because although she looked and sounded all horrified she didn't shout when she asked me, "What the devil have you been up to?"

I mumbled something about getting caught in the bushes while I was playing and mum came straight back at me with, "I suppose you was climbing a tree!"

I just said, "Yes. And I fell out," which was enough to stop her from asking any more questions and she sent me into the house to change my clothes. The first thing I did was to run a bath. Only the one bath wasn't enough and I kept on taking loads of baths, for weeks but nothing I did could make me feel clean.

Even now I can't tell you what it was, but that

experience at Fagley changed me so much I couldn't get close to anyone for years. I couldn't even sit on my dad's knee and have a cuddle any more. Dad kept asking mum what was the matter with me and all mum would every say to explain the change in me was that it had something to do with me going through puberty.

Rape wasn't something you talked about in those days. Not if you wanted to get on with your life. Just reporting it to the police was enough to have everyone looking on you like it was your fault, and lots of people in those days would have looked down on me for the rest of my life.

Then my whole family would have had to live with my disgrace and it was better for all of us if mum never asked. So I never told her, and not telling her broke up that special closeness I'd had at home with my mum and my dad.

When I caught up with Linda I beat the crap out of her, which didn't make me feel any better about what had happened to me and I still couldn't feel really close to anyone. But I did need some kind of friendship and company that would keep me so busy I wouldn't have time to think about what had happened.

I found nearly all of what I needed in the Girl's Life Brigade, whose aim was, *"To help and encourage girls to become responsible, self-reliant, useful Christian women"*. There were always loads of things you could learn and do in the Girl's Life Brigade.

They had a swimming team and I left the Nignogs to compete with them. You could go away with them to camps at the weekends and in the holidays. Some groups had courses in things like photography, music, scripture, millinery, first aid, home nursing, life saving and orienteering.

Our Girl's Life Brigade also had a band that went marching and playing every Sunday. I used to go marching with the band on Sundays and I got to lead it after they found out how good I was with the baton, which I knew how to use from all the practice I'd had with the majorettes after I'd changed my mind about becoming a nun.

There was always something to keep me busy in the Girl's Life Brigade and I'm sure that's what helped me to cope when I lost all of the horses I loved so much and couldn't go riding any more after dad's great uncle at Denholme died, and they sold off the farm to the wrestler Les Kellett.

After that it began to look like what happened to me at Fagley was the start of a long run of bad luck that just would not stop. Shortly after I lost the horses dad's mother got diagnosed with cancer in her muscles and there was nothing the doctors could do for her. Mum and dad moved her in with us and then it wasn't long after that when dad found out he was starting to go blind from Retinal Pigmentosis.

Going blind meant dad had to give up the long-distance driving he loved so much, which got him so down that he stopped being teetotal and he started drinking.

If all of that wasn't bad enough my dad's uncle Charlie at Bradford Waste died, suddenly. He was burping all the time and the doctors were treating him for wind. But one day he came home from work, had his tea, started having his drink, burped, had a massive heart attack and died. It wasn't wind he had at all; it was something to do with his heart.

Dad got even more down when he found out he was having to do loads more of the managing and running the business at Bradford Waste but he wasn't going to get his rightful share of the business until his uncle Gordon retired, which could have taken years.

Everything kept on going downhill with me and the family for the first few years I was at St Blaise and I was beginning to think bad things were never going to stop when I met a lad called Jeff who worked at Brown, Muffs, the big department store in Bradford that some used to call 'the Harrods of the North'.

Jeff was a big, strapping, handsome looking seventeen-year-old lad with a motorbike. I was thirteen at the time, but I looked a lot older than that. The way we met was when a gang of us were splashing and ducking each other in the water at Windsor Street swimming baths and Jeff joined in. Somehow we ended up with splashing and ducking just each other and after that we always seemed to end up swimming and talking on our own.

It wasn't long before Jeff offered me a lift home on his motorbike and in no time at all he was dropping me off at St Blaise, every school morning. Then he started picking me up to take me home and back to school at lunchtimes when mum had to go into hospital to have her varicose veins 'done', because I had all the responsibility for running our home.

As well as going to school I had to do all of the shopping, cleaning, cooking, washing and ironing for all of us. I also had to make sure that dad's 'tea' (evening meal) was always ready and waiting, along with clean and freshly ironed clothes for him to wear when he went to visit mum at night in the hospital, and that carried on the same way when mum went into a Convalescent Home after she got discharged from the hospital.

If it hadn't been for Jeff picking me up and taking me where I had to go, I don't know how I would have managed to keep the home running right. And I think that's the main reason why my parents didn't mind when we started going out in the evenings and at weekends- as long as he brought me back home at the right time.

Getting me back home on time was never easy, because we used to go dancing every Thursday, Friday and Saturday nights at the Mecca on Manningham Lane, where the dancing ended a lot later than my curfew. We still managed to get in a lot of dancing and having a sly drink, though we once got caught drinking underage in the pub.

The police told dad who gave Jeff a 'bollocking' before dragging me up by the ankles and 'clattering' me on the backside, which hurt me even more than it should have, because by then I thought of myself as a grown woman.

But it didn't hurt me enough to stop me from having a drink when we went dancing and by the time I turned fifteen we were so close together that Jeff decided to do the 'right thing', by asking my dad for 'my hand in marriage'.

Dad had no problem with saying yes to our getting engaged and once he'd given his consent we started saving up for our mortgage and getting our 'bottom drawer' together. But I don't think I would have been saving as hard for a mortgage if someone could have told me that less than three years later I would be running away to Scotland. Or that I'd be stopping off at Gretna Green to get married to a workmate, without either of us being in love with the other.

Note:

When I first met my therapist I couldn't talk about the rape without breaking down even though it was 54 years since it happened. So I never said a thing about it to him until we'd been working together for a couple of years. After I did tell him we worked together with one of his therapies called Emotional Freedom Techniques (EFT), which doesn't get rid of the memory but it helped to get rid of so much pain I can talk about it now, without breaking down in tears.

Chapter Five

My last school report from St Blaise said I would never be able to work in an office, but that was their fault and not mine. It was they who made me spend my four years at St Blaise as a free maths teacher to the slower kids, instead of helping me to catch up with my English.

What the nuns didn't realise when they were putting me down was that all the extra maths they'd forced me to do had made me so good with figures that training to be a Comptometer Operator came that much easier to me than it did to most of the others who were training to do accounts at Commercial College.

Being so good with figures got me such a good report I 'walked it' into my first job in accounts at Fosters, the household goods wholesaler on Manningham Lane. Not that I wanted to work in an office on Manningham Lane, or anywhere else. What I really wanted, next to being a model, was to join the

Royal Navy as a WREN and see the world, but my parents wouldn't let me be a model and they wouldn't let me join the Navy. (See end of Chapter for Comptometer description).

Without even asking me what I wanted to do instead of modelling, or joining the Royal Navy they'd just gone ahead and booked me into Commercial College, where they'd paid for a Comptometer Operator course for me and refused to let me do anything else. So I had to be satisfied with working at Fosters, where at least I could finish filling our 'bottom drawer' at trade prices which also meant we could save a lot more money for our mortgage.

Even though it wasn't what I wanted I might have learned to be happy with that if it wasn't for Jeff wanting more out of our relationship. Though I did try to please him every time it started to go that way I would freeze up so much I just couldn't do what he wanted. When I couldn't give Jeff what he wanted he turned on me, threatening me with all sorts of horrible things like how he was going to kill my dog, and when that didn't work he threatened to kill my parents.

Of course I didn't believe he would kill my parents but the way he said it scared me. It was the first time I'd seen that side of him, or anyone else, and he really got to me with all the pressure and threats he kept putting on me. But I still couldn't give him what he wanted, which didn't stop Jeff who kept on and on with the pestering, and the pestering got rougher and rougher until I told him about the rape and how the thought of getting intimate froze me up.

That was the last thing he expected to hear from me and the news shocked him so much he agreed to wait until after our engagement. What I really wanted was to wait until after we got married but that was the best I could get from him and I think I could have forced myself to put up with that if only he'd kept to his word, which he couldn't.

All Jeff managed was a few months before he started his pestering again and then I finally forced myself to give him what he wanted. We were nearly engaged and I didn't want to spoil it all. Jeff had always treated me like a lady and nothing was ever too good for me. Aside from his pestering me for that one thing, the only thing that wasn't completely right with our relationship was Jeff always being a little bit too possessive of me, and once we'd done the deed that side of him went completely out of control.

After that first time Jeff got so jealous of any lad who even 'looked' my way he'd pick a fight with them and that worried me. But I was just fifteen and all of my friends kept telling me Jeff was only doing it because he loved me so much, and because I didn't know any better I just went along with it, which I would never have done if I'd only known just how bad his jealousy would get on the night of our engagement party.

On the night we got engaged our house was full of family and friends from both sides. There was more than enough food and drink as well as music to dance to. Everyone kept saying how beautiful I looked, and how lucky we were, and how we made the perfect couple. I was getting loads of attention from all of the women who all wanted a better and longer look at my dress and my rings.

I was having to spend so much time with the women I barely had a moment with Jeff who still seemed to be having a good time. He was chatting and laughing with the men when I excused myself to go to the bathroom, hoping we could have some time together when I got back.

There was no one on the stairs waiting to use the bathroom so I ran up as quick as I could and I was just closing the door behind me when it was burst back wide open with so much force I was knocked off balance. When I managed to get my balance back I saw Jeff standing in the doorway with a horrible look on his face.

I couldn't understand what he was on about when he started accusing me of ignoring him. I was so confused by his shouting and accusations that all I could think of to say was "Don't be so silly," which made him so mad he punched me so hard in the head I must have gone into some kind of shock.

I couldn't move, I couldn't defend myself and I couldn't stop him when he grabbed me by my hair and smashed my face into the mirror, shattering the glass and making me scream.

This didn't stop him from punching and knocking me round the bathroom until it felt like he was trying to kill me and maybe he would have if dad hadn't run into the bathroom and pulled him off me.

Mum who was right behind dad grabbed me and tried to comfort me as Jeff got dragged to the head of the stairs by dad who was punching him in the back of the head as he pushed him down the stairs towards his mum.

His mum was running up the stairs shouting about how he'd disgraced his family and as soon as she got close enough to Jeff she grabbed him by the front of his shirt, and started dragging him down the rest of the stairs, slapping him across the face while she was dragging him.

When the pair of them got Jeff to the bottom of the stairs they pushed, dragged, punched and slapped him from the front and the back all the way to the front door, where both of them threw him out on the street, slamming the door behind him.

That's the way my engagement ended as soon as it started, with me shivering and crying from shock at the top of the stairs while our families and friends stood for a while in dead silence downstairs. Then they just drifted away without a word.

It was just as well they did because I couldn't have spoken to any of them. I was so devastated by what Jeff done to me that I didn't know what to do. One part of me wanted to run out and ask him to come back. Another part of me wanted to run out and kill him. And another part of me wanted to die of shame.

I couldn't face going downstairs again even when all our guests had gone, so mum and grandma took me to my room and they put me to bed where I could have stayed all of the next day if mum hadn't come up to tell me that Jeff was at the front door, wanting to talk to me.

When she asked me if I wanted to talk to him I said yes, because I had to know why he'd done what he did to me.

After I put the rings back in their boxes I took them downstairs without cleaning up my face or doing my hair and Jeff looked shocked when he saw what he'd done to me.

He couldn't even look at me when he was trying to say how sorry he was. But sorry wasn't good enough for me. I wanted to know the reason why he'd done it and I kept on asking and asking him 'why'.

Even though I kept asking he couldn't give me an answer to the most important thing I had to know. All Jeff could say over and over again was that he didn't know why he'd done it, which was no answer for me and I ended up throwing the box with the rings at him.

Slamming the door in his face should have told him that was the end of any relationship we could ever have, and it would have been the end of it with anyone else but Jeff never really left the house. He just went over the road and stood beside the Ice-Cream Van that was always parked there and he was still standing there when I went to bed that night.

I never found out if Jeff even went home at all because he was still standing there the next morning, in the exact same spot, which was bad enough but it got even worse over the following weeks after he kept turning up in front of Fosters, where he would stand all day and every day I was working. Then he'd turn up outside my home every night, in the same spot near where the Ice-Cream Van always parked up and he was

46

always there the following morning.

Weeks turned to months with Jeff showing up everywhere I went and it got so bad I couldn't go anywhere without looking over my shoulder, which made me so nervous that after a while I couldn't even eat without throwing up.

Then I started getting panic attacks and palpitations all the time, so mum got a Restraining Order against him. But all that made him do was move to the end of the road where the Order ended, and he would always stand where he knew I could still see him.

Before long my nerves got so bad that my mum had to take me to a specialist and my boss got so worried about the state I was in he sent one of the lads at work to pick me up for work and take me home again in the firm's van.

That's when my workmate and myself got talking properly and that's when we found out we had a lot in common. He couldn't get away from an ex-girlfriend who was giving him grief night and day and I couldn't get away from an ex-fiancé who was stalking me into a full nervous breakdown.

Both of us were desperate for a moment's peace and that wasn't going to happen as long as we were in Bradford, so we packed our bags one Thursday and we stole the firm's van after the last person left Fosters that Friday and drove to Blackpool for the weekend. We shared the same room and the same bed in the guesthouse but that was all there was to our relationship, except for us both feeling 'alive' for the first time in months and months.

We felt so 'alive' that we wouldn't have gone back to Bradford ever again but there was no other choice that wouldn't get us arrested for stealing the van and so we drove back to Bradford in the early hours of Monday morning.

As we locked the van back in the garage at Fosters both of us realised we were putting our own selves back into our own prisons which neither of us could bear, so we picked up our suitcases, walked to the coach station and caught the first coach to Scotland.

No one saw us leave and the feeling of freedom as the coach drove out of Bradford kept on growing and growing as the miles went by. The only thing that worried us was that our parents could force us back to Bradford if they ever found us, and the more we thought about it the more we agreed that the only way we could stop them from forcing us back was by taking a diversion to Gretna Green where we registered to get married, even though neither of us was in love with the other.

We had never been intimate but being good friends as well as being in the same situation were more than enough good reasons to try building a new life for ourselves. The only thing standing in our way was that we had to wait for something like two weeks before they would marry us.

While we waited, we used some of our savings to book into a nice hotel and even though there wasn't much for us to do in the way of entertainment, the countryside round Gretna was so beautiful that we spent loads of time going for long walks and having quiet lunches together. Then one afternoon when we were going back into the hotel after a quiet lunch, there was a load of noise and about six cars came flying into the driveway.

I don't know how they found out where we were, but both of our families were there and we were forced to get into different cars while they went into the hotel and got our luggage. I got driven back to Bradford feeling so angry and sad at the same time that I never spoke a word all of the way. There wasn't much point in trying to talk, anyway because they never stopped 'nattering' me all the way home and then they put me in the doghouse for months.

But I didn't care because Jeff seemed to have finally got the message. I did see him hanging around a few more times but he didn't hang around as long as he had been doing earlier and then he completely stopped coming anywhere near the house. He may have hung around Fosters but I wouldn't have known anything about it because Fosters had sacked the pair of us while we were away.

Foster's also sent our wages and holiday pay round to our homes, which worked out really well for me because there was no place for Jeff to hang around and there was no one to tell him where I was working when I got myself another job at Empire Stores.

Note:
The Comptometer was the first commercially successful key-driven mechanical calculator, patented in the USA by Dorr E. Felt in 1887. A key-driven

calculator is extremely fast because each key adds or subtracts its value to the accumulator as soon as it is pressed and a skilled operator can enter all of the digits of a number simultaneously, using as many fingers as required, making them sometimes faster to use than electronic calculators - *Description taken from Wikipedia.*

Chapter Six

Mum and dad put me under 'house arrest' as soon as they got me back from Gretna Green but that ended almost as quick as it started when they realised I would be 'dossing' at home while they were out working to keep me.

When that sank in they put me on 'day release' with orders to get myself a job, which I did with just one visit to Empire Stores where I had one interview on the same day, and the following day I was working for Empire in Accounts.

Empire Stores were a big catalogue company that paid top wages and gave their staff a discount on everything they sold, which made the wages even better. But the best thing of all about working at Empire was meeting and making friends with a girl called Sophie who worked in Commissions.

She was the same age as me and her parents were nearly as strict as mine so we got our heads together and worked out a way to break our curfews. Sophie would tell her parents she was stopping the night at my house, and I would tell my parents I was stopping the night at her house.

It was a simple plan but it worked so well it wasn't long before we were out dancing and having a drink any time we wanted and for as late as we wanted, even though my parents should have known what we were up to because I used to buy a new dress pattern and material every Friday after work and then 'knock up' a dress that night, ready to wear for going out on the Saturday night.

If my parents did know what we were up to they never tried to stop me and for the first time since they forced me back from Gretna Green I began to feel 'alive'. I know I'd been going out at night for a long time with Jeff but being out on the town at night with another teenage girl, meeting lots of new people and making loads of new friends was a lot different to going out with a boyfriend, and I never had such a good time before.

The only time I ever had a bad night out with Sophie was the time we got invited to a 'do' by her brother. Her brother's name was Adam and the football team he played for had won some kind of a Trophy or Competition. The team was having their celebration at Apperley Bridge and Adam had promised us that if we went to the 'do' his friend would give me a lift when I wanted to leave, and he promised his friend would make sure I got home safely.

Adam's friend gave me the lift as I'd been

promised, only the lift ended suddenly when Adam's friend pulled the car over in the middle of nowhere and told me that if I didn't have sex with him I would have to get out and walk the rest of my way home.

So I got out of the car and started walking the rest of the long way home, in the dark, on my own, and I had to walk for ages before I found a phone box.

My dad was sleeping when I rang him up and though he got really annoyed at being woken up to find out I'd got myself into trouble, he did come out to pick me up. And he gave me a right 'bollocking' that ended with him telling me I'd done the right thing.

That was the one and only time I fell for a trick like that, and I was still having a good time going out at night with Sophie when I saw this tall, handsome, well-built, well-dressed lad with 1960s style shoulder length hair in the Beer Keller near Windsor Swimming Baths on Morley Street.

He really stood out from the packed crowd of mostly students and I couldn't help liking the look of him. The only problem was that almost as soon as I saw him Sophie said she was hungry and wanted some fish and chips. I didn't want fish and chips. What I wanted was to wait where I was until I got the big lad to notice me but I couldn't ask Sophie to stay hungry so we left to get our fish and chips.

While we were eating our fish and chips outside the Beer Keller the lad I fancied came out on his own, just as a big gang of lads came walking down the road and they set on him for no reason at all. Though the gang took him by surprise the big lad was fighting back when the police arrived and I don't know why they did it but they picked on him instead of the lads who'd started it all.

One of the 'Coppers' grabbed hold of the big lad by his long hair and the rest of them were helping to drag him to the back of their van. That wasn't fair, so I stuck up for him by shouting at the 'Coppers' to leave him alone, and that he was innocent, but they wouldn't listen to me and when I carried on shouting they warned me to shut up, or I'd be in the back of the van along with him.

If I'd got myself arrested, my parents would have been told what I was up to and that would have been the end of our nights out on the town. So even though the big lad was innocent and the guilty ones were getting away with it I kept my mouth shut while they took him away. But this played on my mind so much for the rest of the night that early next morning I went down to the 'Station' to tell them what had really happened.

By the time I got there they were letting the big lad out without charge and I waited outside until he came out. That's when I found out his name was Derek and he worked for our rival catalogue company which led to us talking some more and to arranging to meet again, which led us to going out nights together.

My nights out with Derek led to a party at his brother's house, where I got so drunk I had to stay the night and we 'did the deed', which led to me getting pregnant from that one time alone. The thought of telling my parents I was pregnant scared me something stupid, but I had no other choice that wouldn't have made it worse for me.

I told mum, who told dad, who disowned me on the spot and ordered me to marry the father. I tried to tell dad that I didn't love Derek and I didn't want to marry him. But all I could get from dad was that it was me who'd dropped my knickers, that it was me who'd made my own bed. And it was me who was going to lie in it, like it or not.

That was all he would say to me and from then on dad refused to talk about anything to do with me. He wouldn't even speak to me at all, and if mum tried to talk to him about me it would always start a big argument between them, which I couldn't stand.

After all it was myself that was pregnant without being married, and it was my fault they were having big arguments. Like it or not I had no other choice than to do what dad said and marry Derek.

He didn't seem bothered one way or another, which didn't surprise me at all when we started to meet his family, who had a very 'different' way of living to us.

If it hadn't been for the 'bottom drawer' I still had from when I broke up with Jeff, and if it hadn't been for mum buying all the carpets, the furniture, the bed, the cot, the cooker and everything else I needed for me and the baby, we would have had nothing at all in that horrible, run down, one outside toilet Council house they sorted out for us on a run down Council estate off Bell Dean Road in Allerton. There, apart from Derek's dad and one of his brothers, most of the family lived from one week's payday or Social money day to another.

When mum saw what I was facing she tried even harder to help me but she still couldn't get dad to change his mind. The only one who might have helped me was my dad's uncle Gordon, if I'd thought to tell him before he was driving me to my wedding.

Gordon must have seen from the look on my face that I didn't even want to go to the Registry Office on Manningham Lane, let alone get married to anyone. But by then I was feeling so hopeless and trapped that I kept telling him I was all right every time he asked me, if I really wanted to go through with it.

That way I lost my last chance to escape from Derek and his 'different' family, who all came back to my parents' house for the free food and drink after the wedding, and when they'd finished enjoying themselves for free they took me off with them to their family 'Do' in the Social Club on their run down estate, where they all seemed to have a really good time celebrating my wedding.

During the 'Do' I forced myself to have a couple of dances with some of Derek's family, including his brother and that made Derek so jealous he set on me when we were walking back home at the end of the night.

At first I couldn't believe it when he turned on me and accused me of trying to 'cop off'' with his brother which was so wrong it was just plain stupid, but he gave me no chance to say anything back before he started 'battering' me, even though he knew I was seven months pregnant.

Now I'm not going to say any more about the 'battering' I took on my wedding night. That would be too much like watching the same film over and over again and I am not going to do that to me or anyone else.

All I will say is that I managed to keep the baby safe from his 'battering' and that he did apologise the next day as well as promising me it would never happen again, which he kept to until I had the baby.

Not long after I'd had the baby Derek came home early one day to tell me he'd given up work because he didn't see why he should be working if I wasn't working. That day was the start of Derek's 'dossing', drinking, gambling and beating me up, which was always worse when he'd spent up all the money and there was no more money to give him.

I did run away to my parents loads of times but that always started more fights between mum and dad. This always made me feel so bad for the trouble I was causing that I always went back to the house on Bell Dean, where loads of times Derek would slap me around for running away and showing him up.

That's the way my whole life was going until I got so fed up and tired of it all that I asked his mother to look after the baby while I went to work soldering television transistors for Baird's at their Beckside Works in Lidget Green.

This changed nothing at all for Derek, who carried on spending his days and nights drinking, gambling and forcing me in bed.

If I'd had somewhere to go I would have left him,

but with dad not wanting me in his house I had nowhere to run and I kept on putting up with it, even though his drinking and gambling got so bad that not long after my second baby I woke one night to find one of his downstairs gambling pals standing in my bedroom doorway.

When I asked the lad what the hell he was up to and what did he want, he told me he was just 'collecting his winnings' and that made me shout so loud that a soldier on leave who was gambling downstairs came running upstairs, grabbed the lad who was stood in my bedroom doorway and threw him out of the house.

This made Derek get even madder with me when he realised he still had to pay off a gambling debt he'd counted on me settling for him in our bed.

Now I don't know and I don't care if he ever did pay the lad off what he owed him. I was working six days a week to put food in our kids' mouths and put clothes on their backs without seeing anything out of it, because Derek would always be waiting outside Baird's on every payday, and I had no choice but to give him my week's wage.

He'd already taken all the Social Security books off me and with my wage gone there was no money to feed and clothe the children. Our gas and electricity were forever being cut off and in the end I had to accept there was no point in working just to keep him in gambling and drinking.

I gave up the job at Baird's and joined Derek on the Social (Unemployment Benefit), which he took off me as well, and that meant the only way I could feed the kids and myself was by taking them over to mum's where she would feed us every three or four days and give me some new clothes for the kids.

Mum always paid for the taxi fare back to Bell Dean but I never had bus fare to get to Gledhill Road and I had to walk nearly five miles there in all weathers, carrying my youngest while I pushed my oldest and heaviest in the pram.

Having to do that time after time, week after week drove me into a deep depression and I don't know what I would have done if it hadn't been for a job coming up in the local Convenience Store, where I could run up a 'tab' and pay it off with my wages, before I got them.

That 'tab' was a real lifeline for me because it meant I could get food every week for the kids, as well as the 'little things' like soap, toothpaste and toilet paper that you can't do without.

Derek used to wait for hours outside the store on payday and when he found out I'd already spent all my wages paying off the 'tab' I'd used for his kids he'd get mad and 'batter' me. But being able to feed my own kids, with my own money made me strong enough to put up with his 'battering' and I was just beginning to find my own self again when everything got a lot harder for my 'real' family.

Dad's uncle Gordon had suffered a stroke the year before my wedding. I think it must have been a mini stroke (TIA) because he'd recovered enough to drive me to the wedding as well as carrying on working, though it seems like he slowly lost interest in running the business which should have led to him letting my dad take it over. But instead of retiring and letting my dad take over the family business Gordon sold it off to Lever Brothers.

He did pay dad his rightful share of the money, and it was enough for him to start his own business trading in 'White Cap' paper with a friend of his. But it wasn't the same as carrying on the family business he'd worked in since he was nine years old, and that got him so far down he ended up spending most of his time in the pub (See end of Chapter for description of White Cap paper).

What with dad spending so much of his time drinking and buying drinks for everyone, he didn't have time to run his own business properly and it was mum who had to help dad's partner to run the 'White Cap' paper business without him. This got even harder when Gordon suddenly died of a heart attack, just before dad's mum tripped over her catheter bag and killed herself by accident.

She'd been sneaking downstairs for a 'fag' (cigarette) in the night for a long time, even though mum had warned her it was too dangerous and she must not do it, because if she fell no one would know and she'd be laid there all night. That's almost exactly what happened, because the fall broke so many bones she died before they found her.

After his mum fell and died, dad's drinking and buying 'drinks for the house' got so bad that by the time I turned twenty-one his 'White Cap' paper business, along with the cars we always owned, the caravan at Flamborough Head and everything else that could be sold was gone.

Dad lost the family thousands upon thousands of pounds that way, and mum was eventually forced to get herself a job as an auxiliary nurse at Leeds Road Hospital, where she later got dad a job as a porter, after he sobered up.

That was a time when I did hope for a while that dad would start talking to me again, but nothing changed. Drunk or sober he wouldn't speak to me and he didn't want me in his house, which they suddenly sold without warning when I was nearly five years into my marriage to Derek.

The first I knew about the house being sold was when mum told me they were going to retire to a bungalow they were buying in Bridlington, and the thought of mum moving so far away from me was devastating. She was the only one who looked out for me whenever she could, and I didn't know what I was going to do without her support.

Then just when I thought I'd run out of hope, the man who was selling the bungalow in Bridlington changed his mind after mum and dad sold their own house, which forced them to find a new home in a hurry. When they found what they were looking for in a bungalow on Elizabeth Drive in Wyke I took what could be my very last chance of getting away from Derek and I moved in with mum, even though I knew my dad didn't want me living with him.

Note:
White CAP paper is described as being low-cost tissue

for wrapping and protection - excellent for packing houseware, china, shoes, etc.

Chapter Seven

From the time I'd been a kid at St Peters' I'd known that every now and again my mum got really bad headaches but I never knew she'd started having blackouts as well until I went to live with her in Wyke.

Mum said they'd sent her all over the place for all sorts of different tests but they still didn't know what was wrong with her and all the different doctors she'd seen had each treated her for something different without making any difference to the headaches or the blackouts.

What was making a difference to the headaches and the blackouts was dad's constant trying to drive me out, which was making mum more poorly. So I went to the Council and they put me on their top-priority-housing-list for being overcrowded with two kids and three adults trying to live in a two-bedroom bungalow.

Even that wasn't enough for my dad who didn't want me at all, and his constant arguing got so bad the only rest we ever had was when he'd gone to work or when Tony came for his 'tea' (evening meal).

Tony worked as a porter with dad at Leeds Road Hospital and when they worked their late shifts together he'd bring dad back to Wyke where first they'd go for a pint in the pub and then they'd come to mum's for their 'tea'.

Though I could see that Tony liked me a lot and he was always nice with me and the kids, I still wasn't free from a bad relationship and I was getting a load of grief from Derek who'd refused to hand the Social and the Family Allowance books back to the Social Security Office.

He kept the books for nearly three months, making me and the kids depend on mum for everything and when the Social did get the books back he turned to mugging me for the little money I was getting.

To this day I don't know how he did it but Derek always seemed to 'know' when I was going to cash in my Social, or my Family Allowance. Every time I went to the Post Office in Wyke he would always be somewhere waiting for me, no matter how often I changed the days.

I would always look to see if he was lurking around and I never saw him when I went in or when I came out with my money, but he was always somewhere close enough to grab me and drag me down a lonely 'snicket' (alleyway), where he would batter me out of every penny.

Then it was back to depending on mum, who did her best but it wasn't fair and it couldn't go on like that.

So I went to see a solicitor who got me Legal Aid and I went for a full divorce.

While I was waiting for my case to come through I "nattered" and 'nattered' the Council until they gave me a home of my own, in the first set of flats that used to be on Eaglesfield Drive, at the top of Woodside Estate, which is just off Halifax Road.

The flat they gave me wasn't furnished but that didn't bother me because there was everything I needed, back at the house on Bell Dean and dad must have been that glad to see the back of me he went and got me a van, which he asked Tony to drive for me and my mum.

She wanted to help with moving all my things but when we got to the house there was nothing left to move because Derek and his 'different' family had stripped the whole house clean. They'd taken the carpets, the curtains, the beds, the wardrobes, the chests of drawers, the kids' cots, the living and dining suites, the children's toys, my clothes, my jewellery and my personal things.

The cooker, the pots, the pans, the kettle, and even the cutlery, plates, dishes, toilet paper and soap were gone. All they'd left in the whole house were some of my kids' old clothes that they'd thrown out of their chest of drawers and left in a pile on the bedroom floor.

Everything I'd ever worked for and everything mum had given me to make us a home was gone and there wasn't a chance of getting anything back because I 'knew' that Derek had sold it all for drinking and gambling money.

The shock of it all must have numbed my brain and I couldn't take it in at first but when it finally did sink in I was so distraught there was nothing my mum or Tony could say that gave me any comfort, even though both of them tried to tell me that everything would come out right and they would help me to get it sorted.

How could I believe that anything would come out right when I'd lost everything I ever owned and I had no money to furnish my flat? Just telling me it would be all right wasn't going to turn an empty flat into a home for me and my kids, and I really don't know what I'd have done if it hadn't been for Tony, who went and asked his own family to help me out.

Tony's parents and five sisters all chipped in with something for my flat. Between them all they gave me everything I needed to move straight into my flat and for the first time in almost six horrible years I had a place of my own where me and my kids could grow and we could live in peace.

Derek did his best to spoil it all by refusing to sign for a quick divorce. But I soon put a stop to that game when I told him if he didn't sign the papers it would have to go to Court, where I'd make sure that everyone in both our families and our kids would be there to hear every single thing he'd ever done to me in detail, and then everyone would know what he was really like and what he'd done to me.

That was enough to scare Derek into signing all the papers and we would have been free of him for good if it wasn't for the Judge, who gave him one day a week's custody, even though we all told the Judge that the children said they didn't want to see their dad any more.

All the Judge kept saying was, "What children wanted wasn't important. Children were there to be seen and not heard," which was such a horrible way to be with children and it was the worst thing he could have done to my kids, because most of the time they'd be all dressed up and waiting for hours before their dad showed up to take them out- if he did remember to come at all.

When Derek did remember, or was sober enough to come and take them out, it was only to drop them off at his mum's while he went off to do his drinking and gambling. And he was nearly always so drunk by the time it came to bring them home that he usually forgot they were with him.

Loads of times the police had to bring my children home because Derek would be so drunk he'd walk off the bus without them, and there were times he'd leave them outside the Betting Shop in Bell Dean while he went in to put on a bet. Then he'd forget they were there and just walk off, leaving them on their own in the middle of the estate.

What Derek was doing to his kids was so unfair I went back to the Court and told the Judge what he was doing, and how anyone could take my kids when Derek left them alone on the bus, or standing outside the betting shop on Bell Dean. But the Judge's mind was set in favour of Derek and he still wouldn't listen.

He let Derek keep taking the kids off me every week and once Derek had what he wanted he began coming less and less often to pick up the children until my youngest went and ruined it all when he opened his mouth about Tony, whom I'd been going out with ever since he'd got my dad's permission to take me to a dinner dance for the staff at Leeds Road Hospital.

On one of the days that Derek remembered to come for the kids my youngest told his dad that he didn't want to go out with him for the day. What he wanted was to wait for 'Tone-Tone' (Tony), and go out in 'Tone-Tone's' car with me, which was enough for Derek to know I had another 'fella on the job'.

From then on I got nothing but more trouble from Derek who went straight for full custody of my kids. I wanted to fight this, but everyone including my parents, my family, my friends and that dickhead of a Solicitor I got through Legal Aid kept telling me to let Derek take my kids.

They all promised me it wouldn't be long before Derek got so fed up of looking after them that he'd be running to give them back and then he'd leave us alone for good. But all of them were wrong and looking back on it all I must have been stupid when I forced myself to believe them enough to hand over my kids without a fight.

After I'd handed them over all I could do was wait for Derek to bring them back as everyone had said he would. And I waited and waited and waited until having to live so close to my kids, without being able to have them at all got to me so much that I knew I had to leave Bradford until Derek was ready to give them back to me.

When I told Tony I was leaving Bradford he gave up his job to come with me and we both put in for jobs with Butlins' Holiday Camps. While we were waiting to hear from Butlins' we bought ourselves an old Vauxhall car that needed working on, and that was all right with me because I'd grown up working on all sorts of cars and engines with my dad.

Tony helped me with stripping the car right down and it was rebuilt and running right by the time Butlins' gave us our jobs at their holiday camp in Minehead. The same day we got our jobs through the post I locked up the flat with everything in it except for my clothes and personal things. Then I handed in the keys for the flat at the Council Housing Office and we drove straight down to Minehead.

The camp was in Exmoor National Park and it was massive. Even though one end was almost on the beach it had a big heated outdoor swimming pool in the park as well as a boating lake with water skiing. There was a monorail to get round the camp, a miniature railway and a chairlift to take you to nature trails. They had a funfair, a cinema, a theatre with live shows every night and theme bars like the Beachcomber where they had all sorts of entertainers and games every night of the week, but we didn't have the time to enjoy it all.

I worked five days a week in accounts and Tony had to work seven days a week as a porter. I had more time to myself, which he didn't like at all and he got more and more grumpy when they wouldn't allow us to stay together in the same accommodation because we weren't married, and it made no difference to them that every night there were nearly as many men in the women's quarters as there were women living in there.

Not being able to stop together bothered Tony a lot more than it bothered me and in the end he spent so much of our time with moaning it got on my nerves. Trying to put up with his constant moaning was really hard work. But I did put up with it until I found out my roommate was taking and using my personal things without asking permission.

Having my personal things used without my permission was the last straw for me, and we went back to Bradford where we stopped with Tony's mum in West Bowling until she got too greedy and started acting stupid. We weren't working, we weren't there half the time and we were having our meals at my mum's but she was still charging us full board just for sleeping there. She was even charging us £2.00 (GBP) to use the washing machine, which was bloody stupid when the take-home pay that I remember from those days was under £50.00 (GBP) a week.

In the end Tony's mum got so greedy I had to stick my nose in and when she said I was only Tony's 'bed woman' we fell out in such a big way that we couldn't stay there any more, so we went to stay with one of Tony's sisters. But Tony went and messed it up when he kept making nasty comments about their dad and in the end we had to leave because of all the arguments he kept causing.

We tried to stay at my mum's but my mum was a 'proper' Roman Catholic who couldn't let an unmarried couple sleep together under her roof. She would have let me stay with her if I was on my own. But I couldn't leave Tony to fend for himself while I slept in a warm bed every night. So we settled for a daily meal and a daily 'wash' while we searched for a place of our own.

Paying so much for everything at Tony's mum had left us short of money so we sold the car for enough to make a rent deposit but we couldn't find anywhere fast enough, and we had to spend our first few nights sleeping rough on the benches outside the public toilets on the patch of green at the top of St Enochs Road, just before Wibsey roundabout.

The weather in Bradford at that time of year had turned so cold, damp and foggy that even when we were cuddled up it wasn't enough to keep warm and we spent most of our days walking round Bradford, searching everywhere we could think of for any place we could shelter at night. Finally we found some new houses they were still building just off Manchester Road.

Every night we'd wait until the builders had all gone home and then we'd sneak into one of the empty houses where we slept on the floor covered up in old papers until we got ourselves a Bedsit on Manningham Lane and then at last we could look for work.

Tony always claimed he was looking for work but he never got a job and he couldn't have tried very hard. There were plenty of jobs about at the time and it wasn't long before I was working back at Empire Stores where I met a girl who was going out with one of Derek's brothers.

The lass let me know that Derek didn't have my

kids at all. He'd just dumped them on his mum as soon as I'd handed them over and he wasn't even giving her any of the extra money he was claiming for them from Social Security and Family Allowance.

She told me it was Derek's mum and dad who were doing what they could for my kids while he was out drinking and gambling away all the extra money. That made me so mad I went back to the Court and that's when I found out my kids had never even got the cards or the presents we'd sent them.

As soon as they'd arrived in the post, Derek had sold all our presents and he must have thrown away the cards we sent them because the kids never saw them. He'd given them 'naff all' for their birthdays or their Christmases and that way they never knew we'd sent them anything.

When the Court found out what he'd been up to they took my kids off him and they gave them back to me. That was the end of my life with Derek, who went so far downhill that he ended up on the streets and in hostels.

He finally died from drink and rough sleeping, which is such a shame because he was such a big, handsome lad who could have done what he wanted with his life if he hadn't wasted so much of it doing his best to ruin mine.

Chapter Eight

Getting my kids back from Derek made us overcrowded in the Bedsit on Manningham Lane and the house the Council gave us on Milner Ing (road), Delph Hill Estate, was perfect for keeping an eye on my mum, who was losing her memory along with the headaches and the blackouts.

I could see mum's bedroom window from my sons' front bedroom window and if her bedroom curtains were closed in the daytime it meant she was too poorly to get up and go to work. Then I knew I had to go down there and look after her, which was all right with Tony who loved the kids and didn't mind taking care of them.

In those days Tony would have done anything for us and we were all getting on so well we decided to marry in 1978 after being together for three years and then there would have been nothing wrong with my life if it hadn't been for mum being so poorly and for Tony not wanting to work.

Tony had got himself a job driving Taxis, but that lasted for only a couple of months before he packed it in for the 'Dole' (Unemployment Benefit) and from then on it was just the odd bit of 'cash in the hand' casual work, otherwise he would spend his time just 'dossing' around. So I kept on 'nattering' him until he got himself a place on a vehicle maintenance mechanic's course at the Government 'Skill Centre' that used to be near the Fire Station on Huddersfield Road.

When Tony finished his training as a vehicle maintenance mechanic his dad went to the firm he drove for and got Tony a full time job servicing the firm's 'artics' (articulated lorries), but that job lasted for only a couple of days before he went back to his old ways that soon turned into Tony doing more 'dossing' about than doing casual work.

We really could have done with the money and Tony was fit enough to work but I had too much on my mind to spend much time 'mithering' Tony about going work because mum had got her memory back and she'd shown me a piece of paper she'd found in dad's pocket. (Note: 'mither' is a North UK saying that means to fuss, pester, or annoy someone).

The piece of paper mum found in dad's pocket had a woman's name next to a phone number and she'd asked me what I thought it meant. I'd told her truth when I said it was obvious that dad was 'playing around', which mum couldn't accept, even though the evidence was there in black and white.

There was no way of telling how long dad had been

'at it' with the woman whose name and number was on the piece of paper, but I knew he'd been stopping out nights for a long time and I think my mum must have suspected he was up to something or why would she have shown me the piece paper and asked me what I thought?

As far as I was concerned it was easy to see that dad was up to no good but mum couldn't or wouldn't accept it. I think that had something to do with dad being the only man she'd ever been with and with mum knowing that she was the only woman he'd ever been with when they got married.

There was nothing on this earth or anywhere else that could have let mum go with another man, so there was nothing in her make-up that would have let her accept that dad wasn't just as faithful, and there was no point in just going on and on with telling her that my dad was 'up to no good'.

So I started asking around and it was worse than I expected. Everyone I spoke to told me my dad had been having one-night stands with loads of women for loads of years, and at the time he was having a full-on affair with a woman called Marion who also worked at Leeds Road Hospital.

That was more than enough for me to throw my dad out of the bungalow. And he must have been that ashamed of what he was doing he went without a fight. But mum never let him reach the front gate before she ran out and dragged him back saying she couldn't do that to my dad. He was nearly blind and anything could happen to him.

Every time I threw my dad out of the house the same thing kept happening and in the end I was forced to realise that mum could never accept that dad would ever cheat on her and all I was doing was putting so much stress on my mum it was hurting her worse than it was hurting my dad.

Hurting my mum was something I couldn't do and I stopped myself from throwing him out for her sake. But I couldn't forgive him for what he was doing to mum and I was still disgusted and angry with him when I had my first and only child with Tony in 1979, just six months before mum died from the brain haemorrhage she had on the day after her 59th birthday.

None of the doctors she'd seen over a lot of years ever suspected that mum had an aneurysm even though her mother and grandmother had both died from a burst aneurysm. One doctor had even treated her for pleurisy and I'm trying to be fair when I say that I'm not even sure they could have found her aneurysm with the equipment they had in the 1970s. So mum ended up having a brain haemorrhage without anyone knowing what had been wrong with her, and with no one being there to help her.

Mum should have been with me when her aneurysm burst because when I'd taken the kids to see her earlier that day I'd asked her to come home with me. We'd been to change the kids' library books in Wyke so we'd popped in to see how she was and if she needed anything doing for her.

Dad wasn't there at the time and mum had told me

he was doing one of his late shifts, so I'd asked her to come with us for her tea and bit of company while she waited for him to come home, but she wouldn't come with us. Mum said there was too much for her to do, like making my dad his tea which was such a waste of her last few hours of life, because the aneurysm burst before dad finally did get home, somewhere between eleven and twelve o'clock that night.

There is no way of telling how long my mum was laid there unconscious before my dad came home and found her. I do know that dad told the police about my brother, whom they went and fetched to the hospital. But neither of them told the police about me at all, and my mum was dead by the time I found out and got myself to the hospital. In all of my life, up to then, that was the most unfair thing my dad and my brother had ever done to my mum and to me.

What with dad cheating on mum for years and with my brother only going anywhere near when he was after money, neither of them should have been anywhere near her when she was dying. I was the one who'd taken care of her and it was myself who'd done everything for mum that she needed.

Yet I was the only one who never got to see her before she died in the hospital which still hurts me to this day, even though I do 'know' that mum waited to say her goodbyes to me because I 'felt her' pass right through my body. And I don't care what anyone thinks, or what anyone wants to believe, because I 'know' my mum waited to say goodbye to me, and I 'know' it was mum who passed through my body.

Mum waiting to say goodbye should have made me feel a lot better about my dad and my brother. But when I'd finished with putting the children to bed that night I looked out the window to say my usual goodnights to her and I was shocked to see the lights were on in the bungalow. I knew that my dad wasn't there and there shouldn't have been any lights.

I thought it must be burglars and we rushed back down to the bungalow where the only burglars we found were my brother and his wife. They were loading up their estate car with things from the bungalow and I asked them what the hell did they think they were up to.

They were so shocked to see me they couldn't wait to drive off and at first I thought we'd caught them in time to stop anyone taking mum's things. But when we went in to check on the house, I found we were much too late to stop someone from breaking into mum's cabinet.

That cabinet was where mum kept all her valuables and important things like cash money for really big emergencies, as well as her Bank books, Post Office Savings book and loads of Share Certificates bought over the years in big companies like ICI, Dunlop, and Empire Stores.

Everything of any value in that cabinet had been taken, along with all the sort of things that no family can ever replace, like Birth, Marriage, Baptism, Christening, swimming, sports, school, and college certificates, along with all of the address books with all of the phone numbers for our family members in

Scotland and Ireland- and I never saw any of it ever again because I think that anything that couldn't be cashed got thrown away by the thieves.

Now I have to say that I can't accuse my brother or his wife of taking anything that was in the cabinet because I never saw them doing it. But 'someone' stole all the valuables and they'd managed to do it in the very short time between me going home and coming back to find my brother and his wife filling their car with things from the house.

Whoever it was that took the money, the share certificates, her bank books and her savings books must have known enough to find and steal mum's Death Certificate, along with the right documents to prove to the banks, the post office, and the stockbrokers that they were the executors because all her accounts got emptied, not long after the night her things were stolen. The thieves sold off all the shares as well, which was so stupid of them because they'd have still been getting paid out every year. So whoever it was that stole most of mum's valuables lost a lot of money that way.

It wasn't the money that hurt me the most. It was the loss of so many personal things that could never be replaced and neither could my mum, who I loved so much that I totally 'lost my rag' when I found out that dad and my brother weren't planning to give her a 'proper' funeral. They were just going to leave mum laid at The Chapel of Rest and let the Funeral Directors get on with her burial.

That wasn't good enough for my mum and it wasn't what she deserved. Mum was a proper Roman Catholic who deserved a proper Roman Catholic funeral with a proper service, followed by a proper Wake, and by the time I got finished with my dad and my brother they'd been down to St Joseph's Church and made all the arrangements, including having the Canon himself to take the Funeral Service.

And I made sure they arranged for a proper 'Wake' after the funeral, so that the whole family could come and say their goodbyes with the proper respect that my mum deserved. That was the very least we could do for my mum and I might have been happy with that if it hadn't been for the Canon going on and on at the Funeral Service about how much God loved us all.

The Canon said it so often I couldn't take it any more and I was loud enough for everyone in the Church to hear when I told him not to be so stupid, and how could he say that God loved us so much when it was God who'd taken my mum away from me.

For a few moments the Canon was shocked speechless, and that's when he should have had sense enough to keep his mouth shut but he didn't, even though he could see how upset he'd made me. I knew from the stupid look on his face he was going to say something just as daft as the things he'd already said, but I never gave him the chance. Before anyone knew what was happening, including me, I was 'on him' and I was still 'clattering' him when the mourners came out of their shock and dragged me off the Canon.

No one could take in what I'd done and I knew he could have called the police for assault, but all he did was mumble something about how he understood and that was the end of his stupid goings on about how much God loved us all. That way mum got her proper funeral and she would have been able to rest in peace if dad hadn't come and told me during the 'Wake' that he was moving in with that slut-whore-bitch Marion he'd been sleeping with.

The thought of dad doing that on the very same day he'd buried his wife made me 'lose my rag', for the second time that day. Everyone at the 'Wake' could hear me when I told him how disgusting he was and what I thought of him for even thinking of doing a thing like that, when his wife wasn't cold in her grave.

Dad tried to defend himself by saying "Well! How long do you expect me to grieve?" And his stupid words were barely out of his mouth when I snatched up a kitchen knife and nearly stuck it into his chest before I was grabbed.

I was that mad I don't know how they did it but somehow they managed to get the kitchen knife away from me and they held me back while they got my dad away. He must have known how close he'd come because his face was 'drip white' when they hurried him through the dead silence in the house.

Once dad was gone and they'd all found out what was really going on, they were just as disgusted as me with him. All of them understood why I'd done what I did and they all stayed to give mum a proper send-off with proper respect.

Chapter Nine

It wasn't long after we buried my mum that dad sold the bungalow in Wyke and some people might find it strange when I say that I helped dad to move in with his whore. But I had to see what it was about her that made my dad choose Marion over my mum and when I did get to meet her I couldn't work out how he even knew what she looked like.

My dad was so blind he could only see faces in 'clips' and Marion's head shook so much it couldn't have stayed in the same place long enough for him to work his way down her face, which wasn't a patch on my mum's and neither was anything else.

Saying that about Marion isn't being nasty to her. I know what it's like to be really disabled and I know how cruel other people can be when they think they're 'normal' and you are not. So I'm only telling it like it was when I say that Marion's home was a 'state' with its tired old settee and worn out carpets.

There was no need for Marion's home be in a 'state' like that. I've spent over 20 years with mostly only the one good leg and mostly with only the one good arm but I've always somehow managed to keep a clean and tidy home, mostly on my own.

I've always had to struggle but I've always found ways to do my own cooking, cleaning, washing up and laundry, which gives me the right to say that the way Marion lived and the 'state' of her home were a real disgrace to my mum and the homes she'd made for my dad, but if that was what he wanted, then he was more than welcome to have it.

I had no time for sympathy because the same breathing problems that tried to kill me as a kid came back so bad it felt like my chest was being crushed, and I almost couldn't breathe at all when they rushed me into the hospital where they said it was Pneumonia.

For the next 2 - 3 weeks they put me on a big Oxygen Tank the staff nicknamed 'Big Bird'. While I was on the Oxygen tank they gave me loads of injections and different tests. Some of the tests were for allergies and when all the results came back they told me I had Asthma, for which they gave me some inhalers.

Now that I'm looking back on it all I'm not sure they really knew what was going on with my breathing, because I kept having to go back to the hospital and to the doctors for loads of checkups and tests, none of which was ever going to give them the real reason for my Asthma which I think was from me being unable to accept that mum had died.

I also think that was the same reason why I couldn't talk to anyone any more. It was all right if I was taking one of the kids to school and I only had to say good morning to someone, but if they caught me up and wanted to talk I couldn't string two words together.

Every time I tried to make a proper sentence it was just a load of gibberish that came spilling out of my mouth. When they asked me if I was all right I really had to struggle just to say that I wasn't used to talking to people, and then I'd get away from them as quick as I could.

It all seems so weird when I'm thinking about it, now but it got so bad I more or less locked myself away in the house and when I did go out I couldn't face talking to anyone. I think that must have been because I didn't want to hear any sympathies, or condolences, or anything that would remind me of my mum.

Any time I saw someone coming towards me I would cross the road just in case they tried to talk to me, and if anyone I knew was in the shop I'd wait outside until they were gone before I would go in. If it hadn't been for me finding out there was no headstone on mum's grave and there were no plans to get one, I could have stayed like that for years without talking to anyone except for Tony and the kids.

Just the thought of mum having no headstone made me swallow my pride and I went to my dad, who I had to bully into getting mum a headstone and even then I had to go with him to make sure he didn't get her any old crap.

Forcing my dad to get my mum a decent headstone

got us talking again and I started taking him to places he needed to go like hospital appointments and other important things he had to do. If I was round their house when Marion wanted her shopping I used to take her to get it, but then Marion got so jealous of dad getting on so well with me that she did her best to drive us apart.

Marion would tell dad that I'd said this and that about him and though it was all lies it kept making him fall out with me. Then we were 'on' and then we were 'off', which happened so often I never knew where I was with him and while all of that was happening with dad, I was finding out more and more about the real Tony who'd been hiding away for all those years before mum died and dad sold the bungalow, leaving me with nowhere to run.

Tony had always made fun of me over simple things, but when I had nowhere to run it got so bad that nothing I did was ever right. He was forever calling me thick, stupid, and dumb, and he used to go on and on with saying the same old stuff, over and over again.

It's only now since I did a lot of thinking about how I got to where I was that I've realised the way Tony used go on and on about stuff was a type of brainwashing. He was always putting a thought in your head before something happened, and that's how he'd always got his own way.

Behind that loving but lazy front Tony always showed to the world there was a vicious, cold, calculating, manipulating bastard who planned everything so well you could never see it coming and when it did come, you never knew what was really happening.

Tony was so sly he even found a way to use his own inadequacies against me. After I'd got so fed up with his boring, 'wham-bam-thank-you-mam' ways in the bedroom I'd asked Tony if we could try something different for a change. Instead of talking with me about it he'd gone and told his parents I was a nymphomaniac. This was the last thing he should have said to his mum who didn't like anything at all to do with the bedroom.

Tony's mum liked that side of marriage so little his dad never got any bedroom stuff from her. So they were always going to say something horrible when he told them I was a nymphomaniac. And whatever they were going to say about such a personal thing it was always going to make me feel small, which I now realise is why he'd done what he did to me.

That was just one of the bigger things Tony did to steal my self-confidence from me and for every big thing he did to control us more and more of the smaller things kept creeping in. The worst of them were mostly hidden in the ways he used the love between me and the kids and the love they had for each other.

Any time one the kids told me Tony had done something horrible I'd ask him what was it for and why had he done it, for which he would always 'batter' me first for asking, and then he'd 'batter' the one or the ones that had told me. But there was the time he slipped up with how far he went with his 'battering', and that time it nearly cost him his life.

We'd been arguing over something horrible he'd done with the kids and he'd followed me into the kitchen. He wanted to hit me with a chair but I got a knife before he could land the chair and when he saw the knife coming to get him Tony tried to hide behind the first door out of the kitchen.

There were two doors leading outside from the kitchen with an under stairs cupboard between them. He must have thought he was safe when he managed to shut the first door against me but it was only a cheap, Council House, inside door and I stabbed the knife straight through it, over and over again, cutting up the front of his jacket before he could get away.

Tony ran outside and he roamed around until I went to bed. Even then I made him wait for more than half an hour before I turned the lights out. Then he still waited another half hour or so before he sneaked back in and crept into our bed with me pretending to be asleep.

Most of the time it was mental and emotional cruelty that Tony used to control us. Like all the times he'd give me one stupid excuse or another for sending the kids so early to bed they'd miss their favourite T.V. programmes, especially when they were all excited.

Those were just some of the ways I now know that Tony used to control us all, and if I had seen the truth in those days, I would have known what to do when my oldest said Tony had seriously 'interfered' with her, which is not the way she put it, but that's the most I'm going to say about what she said he'd done to her.

Tony denied it all to me as well as to the Police and

the Social Workers, though none of us could ever get to the truth because first she said he had and then she said he hadn't. Then there were things she did that only made sense if he hadn't. Like the time I was showing her how to do something in the kitchen and she told me she had to go to the toilet, or it was something like that.

She was away for so long I went to look for her and I found her in the living room, sitting on Tony's knee, with both of them looking through a catalogue. There was another time I got so worried for my daughter that I asked Auntie Jessie if we could stop with her. But we were there for only a couple of days before my eldest said Tony had never done anything at all to her and she said she wanted to go back home.

To this day I do not know if that was the truth, or if it was something to do with Auntie Jessie not having a television. Even the police and Social Workers were having such a hard time getting to the truth of it all that one detective told me he didn't think Tony had ever done anything at all to her but in the end they took her away from me for her own safety and they put her in a Home at Guisley.

Putting my daughter in a home at Guisley didn't make it any easier to work out what had really happened between her and Tony - or if anything at all had happened - because she was still going to school in Wyke and when she came over to have her lunch with us she would tell us that she was soon coming home.

When I went to the Home and talked to the woman who ran it she said she knew nothing about it and then the next thing I knew my daughter wanted to go and live with a friend of hers whose dad owned a nightclub. They had a lot of money and the dad said he'd adopt her but when the police and Social Workers looked into it all they found he had a prison record.

That was the end of her friend's dad adopting my daughter, but there must have been something about her that others could see as well as me, because two of her social workers that were married and lived in a big house fostered her, and she was still living with them when my breathing got so bad I couldn't walk up the hill to the house.

I had to keep stopping every few steps to catch my breath and my doctor wrote me a letter to the Council. They gave us a house on Buttershaw where it was flat, but they couldn't give me what I needed most because all the while my daughter was growing up without being in my life.

It was probably safer for her that way because there came a time when Tony got sent to prison for tying up a prostitute with wire and raping her at knife-point, which makes me believe he did what she said he did but by then it was too late to help her and I can't go back in time to put any of it right.

Chapter Ten

T he problems I had with talking to people got sorted when my youngest son Philip started his first school, at the back of Reevy Crescent. Having to take him to school every day forced me into talking to the other parents and his teachers. Though it was really hard for me at first, the more I talked the easier it got and it wasn't that long before I could string a full sentence together.

Being able to hold a proper conversation gave me enough of my old confidence to go down to the Social on my own and ask them for the money to get a new bed, because by the time we moved to Buttershaw the bed we had was so old and tired it was giving me horrible backache.

I didn't like having to go to Social for help but with Tony being too lazy to stick to a full time job, and with me having really bad Asthma as well as the kiddies to look after, we never had any money. So the only way to get rid of my horrible backache was 'talk' the Social into giving me the money, which I did.

The money I managed to get from the Social was only enough for a really cheap bed, which wouldn't have helped with my back. So I took the money to The Bed Shop at the top of Sunbridge Road and I used it to make a deposit on a really good bed. Then every time I went in to pay off my 'tick' I'd 'mither' George Harrison about giving Tony a job.

George Harrison owned The Bed Shop and I don't know if he really wanted to take on anyone else, or if he just wanted me off his back but either way he did give Tony a job delivering beds and keeping up with the stock in the 'warehouse' they had above the shop.

In no time at all Tony was making up to a £1,000 every few months in bonus on top of his regular wage. That was really good money for the early '80s in Bradford, and what with Tony being at work all day I had enough of my own space and my old confidence back to start making friends with a girl I'm going to call Ann.

My eldest lad Mark and Ann's lad had made friends when my eldest started at Buttershaw School on Reevy Road West. The two were always playing together and my youngest used to hang around with them. That way me and Ann were forever meeting up and we soon got talking, as you do.

Ann was making extra money for her and her kiddies by doing ear piercings and holding clothes parties in other peoples homes for a firm called 'It's a Pleasure', which later changed its name to 'Glad Rags'.

I'd wanted to get my ears pierced for ages and my birthday was coming up so I got Ann to do it as my birthday present to myself, and it was then that we had our first real conversation.

After a while we started talking about more personal things and I found out that Ann's husband was a right bastard, like mine. But I never realised how bad he was until one day I just knocked on their back door and walked in to find him with a knife against Ann's throat. His other hand had her by the neck and she couldn't get away.

I warned Ann's husband to leave her alone and he warned me to get out of the house or he'd cut my throat open along with hers, and I had no reason not to believe him. It was a chance I couldn't take, so I ran to a phone and called the police who came and took him away.

After the police had taken her husband away I rang up the Social for Ann and they gave me a list of 'safe houses', which I rang around until I found one that could take her in. Then I went and got Tony's dad to drive us all to the 'safe house' where she stayed for only a little while before she went back to her husband.

When Ann came back to Buttershaw she told me she was going to start her clothes parties again and she asked me if I wanted to join up with her. At first I was too nervous but the more I thought on it the more I could see a way of making my own money and in the end I told her 'yes'.

It was through us holding our clothes parties in other peoples' homes that we started meeting up with more girls from Buttershaw who were also doing clothes parties for 'It's a Pleasure'. We all got talking about what we were doing and most of us agreed that we'd be a lot better off if we all worked together, but we needed a place to hold our meetings and it was Ann who got us a room to rent in the Ring 'o' Bells pub in Halifax.

After our first meeting was over me and Ann went for a drink in the bar where there were two, well dressed, good looking lads having a drink and - to cut a long story short - Ann and one of the lads got together, leaving the other lad on his own at the bar. He spent so much of his time staring at me that I went and asked him, "Why don't you come over and join us. Instead of just standing and staring at me."

He took me up on my offer and he turned out to be best friends with the lad that Ann had taken a liking to. He was divorced and he worked as a Company Director but the thing I liked about him the most was that he treated me like a woman instead of an idiot, like Tony always did with me.

That lad was everything my husband Tony wasn't and I really liked him a lot but I was a married, Roman Catholic lass and talking was as far as it could go, which wasn't the same for Ann who had no problem with starting up an affair.

Ann and her new boyfriend used to meet up in the Ring 'o' Bells and I'd go along with her to make up a foursome with my Company Director who always wanted to sit and talk with me and I couldn't understand it. After all, he was a smart, intelligent man

94

in charge of a firm full of intelligent people while I was only a 'thick, dumb and stupid' woman and the time came when I had to ask him why he wanted to talk to a 'thick, dumb, and stupid' person like me?"

I was so surprised when he told me I wasn't like that at all and if that's what my husband told me then he was wrong. This was a really big shock to me because from the time I'd been a kid the nuns at St Blaise had always told me I wasn't clever enough to work in an office, and that was long before Derek, then Tony had 'battered' and 'nattered' me into believing I was 'thick, dumb, and stupid'.

That wasn't the only shock I got because next time we met he told me he'd applied for a new job as a Company Director with another firm. He said they'd asked everyone who was after the job to draw up a business plan that showed how they'd improve the business and I was amazed when he told me he wanted my opinion on his plan. But I went through it, anyway and when I'd finished he asked me what I thought.

I told him it would be their loss if they didn't take him on, and he told me that was exactly the same thing his mother had said, which gave me such a lift I knew I could make a success of the clothes parties, even after most of the other girls had lost interest and slowly drifted away.

I told Ann what I thought about carrying on and she felt the same way as me so we designed our own leaflets and started leaving leaflets all over the place as well as getting new girls interested in holding clothes parties for us.

Our recruiting went so well for us that we soon took over from where the other girls had left off and that got us working more closely with 'It's a Pleasure', who got us to go around and collect all their stock from the other girls.

Most of the stock we collected was in a horrible state and some of it was so full of infestations that we ended up burning or throwing nearly all of it away, but we still had enough to start arranging our own fashion shows, to promote our clothes and to get more girls interested in holding more parties for us.

Our first fashion show, if I remember it right, was in Sowerby Bridge the other side of Halifax. I did all the modelling the way Aunt Jessie had taught me, and we ended up getting some new girls that were interested in holding clothes parties for us. Then we started going to different Shows and Conferences, looking for new materials, new styles and all that sort of thing.

One way or another we were always out doing something for the business which Tony didn't like me doing, even though I always made sure his 'tea' was ready for him, just to dish up when he got home from his work. But always having his 'tea' ready and my making money out of my own hard work wasn't enough to stop him from accusing me of having affairs.

He was always accusing and 'battering' me for having affairs I wasn't having. I wasn't doing anything wrong and in the end I got so fed up of his accusing and 'battering' me I thought to myself, 'what the Hell! If that's what Tony thinks of me then I might as well have the affair'.

That was the start of my affair with my Company Director, and I do have to say I enjoyed every moment of our affair which went on for a long time without Tony ever having a clue. The only reason it ever ended was through me being too afraid of hurting the kids.

Looking back on it now, I wish I'd done the same as Ann who eventually left her husband for the lad that she met in Ring 'o' Bells pub in Halifax. They ended up getting married and the last time I saw her she was having a good life with him, so I think I let myself down by saying no to my Company Director when he wanted me to leave Tony for him.

We did stay really good friends when our affair was over and I also have to say that he was the one who got me to believe in myself again. But I'm getting too far ahead of myself because we were still having our affair when Tony got me a full-time job through a 'Rep' he met in The Bed Shop.

The 'Rep' was a regular in The Bed Shop and one day he asked Tony what I did. Tony told him I was a Comptometer Operator and I needed a job. The 'Rep' told Tony he knew of a firm that probably needed one and he gave Tony a number that I rang the very next day.

The number got me talking to an accounts firm called AlphaCal and they asked me to come in for an interview. This must have gone well because they asked me to start the following day doing 'Costings' at Dean Clough Mills Business Centre in Halifax.

We all had to take our turns on Reception and I didn't mind because of all the different and interesting people it gave you the chance to meet. One of the interesting people that were always popping in and out was Sir Ernest Hall, who owned Dean Clough Mills. He'd rescued the derelict mill and turned it into a Business Centre with an Art Gallery.

Sir Ernest Hall is a lovely down-to-earth man who always found the time to stop and have a little chat with you, even when he was with Prince Charles who used to visit every now again. I think it was the new Art Gallery along with some of the other new things in the Mill that Prince Charles came to see with Sir Ernest Hall.

Whenever they came to visit they'd always come into the Mill by the 'quiet way' through the back door by the car park, and that meant they had to pass through Reception. That's how I got to see so much of Prince Charles who was always nice with the way he would have time to stop and have a little chat with anyone he met on his way. And who you were or what you did for a job never seemed to make a difference to either of them.

I can't be sure any more but I think it was somewhere round 1985 that Prince Charles and Sir Ernest Hall used to visit the Mill together. In those days, I used to go to work on the bus but by then myself and Tony were bringing in enough money between us to run a car so Tony went to his dad and we bought the Midnight Blue, 1600 Ford Cortina his dad was going to exchange for a Brown 2 Litre Ford Cortina.

I loved that Midnight Blue 1600 Ford Cortina so much I named her 'Black Beauty', and just owning 'Black Beauty' wasn't enough for me. I needed to drive her on my own and I started having 'proper' driving lessons with a retired 'Traffic Cop' who'd set up a driving school in Wibsey.

Ann was also letting me drive her car to and from our regular 'meetings' in the Ring 'o' Bells and I was getting so much practice with my driving that I passed my test first time. Then I was driving 'Black Beauty' to work at Dean Clough Mills as well as going out for AlphaCal.

Most of the other girls didn't like going out of the office and in that way I was different because I loved getting out and about, seeing new places and meeting new people and it was while I was out doing an audit at Empire Stores that I saw how much they were paying AlphaCal for our services.

AlphaCal were getting so much for the machine and so much for me but what I was getting for doing the work was peanuts to what they were making off me and that wasn't fair, because I was the one that was killing myself for the little bit of money I was getting out of it.

The more I thought about it the more unfair it looked to me and the more unfair it seemed to me the more convinced I was that I could do it on my own. But when I told Tony I wanted to start my own business he just laughed in my face.

Tony laughing in my face wasn't enough to put me off and I started talking to some of the other girls at Dean Clough Mills. When I told them what AlphaCal was charging the clients and what we were getting out of it, they all thought it was just as unfair as I did which got us on to talking about setting up on our own.

All the girls were all 'yeah, yeah, yeah' so we set up a meeting at one girl's house and it was all 'yeah, yeah, yeah', again. It was all noise and nothing ever came of it, but that didn't make me want to give up and I still wasn't going to give in when I met up with a girl called Carol who lived in Wakefield.

I'd never seen Carol in Dean Clough Mills but she had worked for AlphaCal who'd phoned her up to ask her if she'd go over to Empire Stores where they'd just sent me back for another audit, and that's how we got to know each other.

One day I told her how I'd tried to set up an accounts business with the other girls at Dean Clough Mills and I told her how the girls had been all talk and no action. When Carol heard what I wanted to do she saw it the same way that I did. She got so excited about the idea we got together and sent out letters to different firms offering the sort of accountancy service we both thought they might need.

Carol's husband designed the letters and I typed them out. We sent the letters all over, without getting much response until one day Carol's husband rang her at work to tell her he'd had a telephone call asking us to audit a firm called G.T. Smith's.

When we looked into G.T. Smith's we both got right excited. They were a family-owned chain of supermarkets and their main offices were based in Knottingley. If I remember it right they had supermarket branches in Pontefract, Castleford, Meanwood, Outwood, Normanton and Ossett.

Two brothers had built up the chain from one

butchers shop that their father had started. They were famous for the freshness of their produce. Their meat was beautiful. They had their own bakery at Townville in Castleford. We couldn't have wished for a better start and we took the audit on.

The audit went well and we must have done a really good job because when we'd finished it one of the brothers came down to see us. He asked us if we'd do it again and he said they had two audits a year. One of their audits was in April the other was in October and we said yes to both of them.

Doing the books for G.T. Smith's got us friendly with some of the girls who were working there. They told us how the other firms who'd being doing their auditing were always letting them down, and they told us about some other firms that had been let down as well. So we got all their information and details from the girls and then we sent out letters to them.

When they found out we were doing the books for G.T. Smith's they gave us their business as well, and we were soon making really good money. But it was really hard work keeping up with all the audits because I was still working for AlphaCal at Dean Clough Mills.

The only way I could audit our clients as well as theirs was by me taking the time off work, and I used to give AlphaCal excuses, like one of the children were sick and other things like that. After a while AlphaCal started bringing their work to me at my house, and I would do the work for them at night. They never complained or pulled me up about taking so much time off work, which meant I must have been doing a good job for them as well as for our own clients. But all that extra work took up so much of my time I had to make a choice between my new business and the clothes parties.

I knew I could make a lot more money out of our accounts, and I had no other choice when I 'knocked the clothes parties on the head' but I stayed good friends with Ann who was happy for our success- which wasn't the same with Tony.

When Tony saw the amount of money I was bringing in he wasn't laughing any more. But instead of being happy with our success like Ann was, it only made him more jealous of me. When anyone said how well I was doing he'd give me a right thumping as soon as he got me on my own, and that's one of the reasons why it came as such a big shock to me when Tony told me he wanted to go into business with me!

Chapter Eleven

The reason I agreed to go into business with Tony was because of my kids. I'd already made up my mind to divorce Tony before he'd even asked me and I'd been saving every penny I could for when I left him. Going into business with Tony was another opportunity for me to give my kids a better life than the one I could give them as a single mum.

Whatever was going to happen between us I would still own 50% of any new business and I couldn't deprive my kids of what that extra money could do for them once we were on our own. So I'd said yes to Tony and then he went to his mum for the money.

Tony was his mother's favourite and there was nothing wrong he could do in her eyes. She would have done anything for him and she had no problem in getting him the money by putting a mortgage on the house that Tony's dad had left her after he'd died in November 1989.

When the mortgage money came through we went to an Estate Agents that specialised in businesses and it's a good job Tony had his dad's 2.0 Litre Ford Cortina by then because he didn't have the first clue about anything to do with finding, starting, or running a business and that meant I needed 'Black Beauty' for all the running around I was forced to do, between Alphacal, my clients and finding our new business

If Tony did get involved he didn't know what he was talking about and nothing sensible ever came out of his mouth. That's why all the owners of all the businesses we were looking into and the Estate Agents did all their talking to me, which made Tony so jealous of me that every single time we got into the car, after we'd had a meeting it was always "He fancied you," from Tony and then he would always 'batter' me, for his imagination that all the men we'd been talking to had all been 'chatting me up'.

His jealousy got so bad he was even claiming that the man who owned the Estate Agency fancied me and in the end I got so fed up of his accusing and 'battering' me that after a meeting we'd had with a woman who'd done all the talking to me, I'd asked Tony, "Well? Is she a Lesbian, then?"

Tony's answer to that was to give me a right thumping when we got home and I think it was then that I realised Tony's real problem was that he was insecure and inadequate. Everything Tony had ever done to me had been to steal my self-confidence, just to make him feel like he was a 'somebody' and I know that's the truth because the more successful I'd become, the more abusive and impotent he'd be until raping was the only way he could 'perform' with me.

What I never realised was that my eldest son always heard what Tony was doing to me and I can't say what I'd have done if I'd known at the time that my son was having to lie there and listen to Tony raping me.

All I can say is that seeing Tony clearly for the very first time made me even more determined to leave him and that's why I put everything I could of myself into finding us a business that I knew we could succeed in, even though the partner I was stuck with knew nothing at all about business and didn't have the type of brain for it.

But I had that type of brain and it was in my own interest to make sure I'd end up owning 50% of a business with a really good profit margin. That's the reason why I looked into businesses like a Florist Shop and a Card Shop. I knew that Card Shops could make a 100% profit and I was really tempted to go for the one we were looking into- until a Café came up for sale.

I'd worked in mum's aunties' Café from when I was just a little kid, and I knew we could make a lot more money out of a Café than we could out of a Card Shop though there were a couple of Café's, a Sandwich Shop and a Fish and Chip Shop near the Café, which was just off Queens Road in Halifax.

Having so many food places so close together might have put someone else off from buying the Café but I didn't look on the others as competition. What I saw was a popular and handy place for lots of people wanting something to eat and I knew if the food we did was better quality and value than all the others in the area, it would be our Café that would get the most custom. So I went round and tasted the food in all of the other food places in the area and once I'd done that I knew I could do a lot better than all the others. This was enough for me to go for the Café.

First I needed a closer look into the Café before we bought it and when we went round the premises I could see it needed a lot in fixtures and fittings. Then I had to run round all over the place, looking for bargains and pricing up everything we needed.

We were due to sign the papers on Saturday the 3rd of November 1990 and I had everything sorted by Wednesday the 31st October which just happened to be Halloween. But I never got to sign the papers because my aneurysm burst and I brain haemorrhaged at 10.15 p.m. that Wednesday night which was only eighteen days after my 39th birthday and just 3 days before we were due to sign for the Café.

We'd spent most of that Halloween day finalising the deal on the Café and I'd had my own work to do, as well. By the time I'd finished it was late and they told me I was turning to get a spoon for a Yoghurt I'd just got out of the 'fridge when I put my hand to my head, screamed, and fell to the floor unconscious.

They said that after I screamed and fell unconscious Tony picked me up off the floor and laid me on the living room couch while he tried to bring me round by slapping my face.

Slapping my face to bring me round from a stroke

was the sort of stupid thing that Tony would do and my head was rocking from side to side all the way to the Casualty at the BRI (Bradford Royal Infirmary), where my head kept on rocking from side to side and the top of my head kept swelling up until it was massive.

I was lucky enough that a young doctor working in Casualty diagnosed me with either a brain haemorrhage or a brain infection. He called for his boss, Dr Shaw, but before he arrived they'd got me stabilised enough to transfer me onto Ward 5 where the next doctor who took care of me was Dr J Wright and they said that he and his Staff Nurse Sian took so many blood and other tests that by the time Dr Shaw arrived on the Ward I looked like a pin cushion.

Dr Shaw must have been at a 'Do' because they said he arrived on the Ward wearing a Tuxedo. I don't know if Dr Shaw ever knew I was a cousin of his, through him being a son of dad's Uncle Gordon, though the luckiest part of that coincidence was Dr Shaw knew Mr Towns, the Neurological Surgeon at Pinderfields Hospital at Wakefield.

Pinderfields was not only a top Neurosurgery hospital but Mr Towns is also one of the very best Neurosurgeons in the whole country so I couldn't have got luckier than Dr Shaw phoning Mr Towns to ask him if he would accept me to go there. Mr Towns is such a nice and caring man he agreed to operate and I don't know if I could hear the Ambulance Siren going off while I was being rushed to Pinderfields, but to this day I get a really weird and sickly feeling every time I hear an Ambulance Siren.

My therapist told me he doesn't know if it's true, but some people say a person's hearing is the very last thing to go, which might help to explain that feeling I get when I hear an Ambulance Siren.

The most important thing is that the Ambulance got me to Pinderfields in time for them to operate and while they were operating on my brain Tony and his mum were off signing the papers for the Café, even though they didn't know if I was going to come out of the operation alive or dead, or like a baby, knowing nothing at all for the rest of my life, either of which could have happened to me because I had another stroke while I was on the operating table.

The second stroke collapsed my lungs and stopped my heart, and when they'd managed to sort all of that out, Mr Towns Understudy had so much trouble with 'clipping' the aneurysm that Mr Towns had to take over.

And from now on it's up to you to believe what you want to believe, because a strange thing happened to me during the operation.

I know that my eyes were open while I was on the operating table, because after I got discharged from the BRI and I was going for my checkups the first thing Mr Towns' Understudy said to me when I sat down in his office for the first time was, "I see that you've still got those beautiful blue eyes! And I thought- "Bloody hell! No wonder you had so much trouble with clipping my aneurysm if you were gazing into my eyes!"

Anyway, while I was on the operating table I felt as if my head was clamped tight in a way that forced me to look up at the operating theatre light and all the edges round my sight were hazy like there was some sort of interference.

I could just make out what I thought were nurses and other people moving around me and then the operating light got brighter and brighter; as it got brighter and brighter, it was pulling away, pulling away, but even though it went right back, it left a really bright light that I thought I could feel all the way round my face.

The light was stronger in the middle and that's where I was looking when I saw my mum and my father-in-law (Tony's dad). I could see that mum was beckoning me in the same way she used to do with her hand when it was time for me to stop playing and come in. Then both of them started telling me that if I stayed where I was I would have to go through a lot of pain and I would be better off if I went with them.

Both of them kept on telling me that, and mum kept on beckoning me but I 'knew' without a thought in my head that I couldn't do what they asked and both of them left, with Tony's dad 'tipping' the side of his forehead with the first two fingers of his right hand like he always did when he said goodbye to me, and that's how I was sure it was him that I'd seen.

As for me, I 'stayed' where I was and it was thanks to Mr Towns that my life was saved. The one 'catch' to staying alive was that my family got told I would have to spend the rest of my life laid flat on my back in bed.

Everyone else thought the same when I got transferred from the Operating Theatre to Intensive

Care in Pinderfields, where I stayed on life support until I was breathing well enough to be put on a machine that took over if my own breathing stopped.

They kept me on that machine in Intensive Care at Pinderfields until I'd gone for a few days being able to breathe on my own without needing the machine to 'kick in'.

Once I was able to breathe on my own, I got transferred to Intensive Care at the BRI and it was while I was laid there unconscious that I saw a lot more of mum and Tony's dad.

They were always 'nattering' me to come with them and they would always tell me if I didn't come with them I would have to go through a lot of pain and suffering but I always 'knew' that I couldn't go with them.

One day I sort of 'came to' and I could only see in black and white when I opened my eyes. The centre of my vision was clear, but all round the edges it was hazy like there was still some sort of interference and I couldn't really see very much but for some reason, I thought I was in a room full of pipes.

I could hear all sorts of 'clunking' noises going on which might have been trolleys with drinks or something being wheeled about on the Ward. Then I could see this figure, and I don't know if I said 'what are you doing', or whether I 'sussed' it out in my own mind, but I suddenly knew that the figure was washing me. I just felt relaxed and I wasn't frightened at all, and then I 'went off' again.

The next thing I remember is that it felt like they

were moving my bed and I can't say if that was when they first transferred me back to Ward 5, or when they were moving me closer to the Nurses Station to make it easier for constant observation.

While I thought they were moving me I'd 'come to' enough to ask them where I was and one of the people moving me said that I'd been poorly, and I remember someone saying I'd be laid on my back for the rest of my life to which my first and only thought was, "I won't let my body do that to me" and then I 'went off' again.

'Coming to' and 'going off' like that happened a lot to me and nothing 'flowed' at all. Looking back on it all is like looking at 'snapshots' where you don't always know which picture was taken first. That's why I can't be certain of everything in order, but the next 'snapshot' I remember is waking up to hear Tony and his mum, so I said "Hello Tony. Hello mum."

I always called Tony's mother 'mum' and after they heard me speaking they both sounded excited when they were saying "Oh! She remembers us! She remembers us!" and then I was 'off again'.

The next time I 'came to' I could hear voices I knew belonged to my kids', Tony, and his mum. They were asking the nurses how I was and I asked them what plane they'd come in on. And what time did it land.

Both Tony and his mum sounded like they thought I'd lost my mind when they asked me what I was on about, and I wish I could have seen their faces when I told them "Well I've just landed. I've been with the 'Busby Babes."

In case you don't know it, the 'Busby Babes' were

the 1958 Manchester United Football team that lost eight of their players in the plane crash at Munich which caused the death of 23 of people on the plane, and I'd just got back from having a right party with the eight players who'd died.

After the plane had landed I was the only one out of the nine of us who had to get off and just a moment before I 'came to' the eight players I'd been partying with were waving me goodbye through the plane doorway and windows.

I could tell that Tony and his mum really believed I'd 'lost it', so I reeled off the names of every single one of the eight dead players I'd been partying with, which was really weird, because it turns out I was only about seven years old when the plane crashed.

But I did grow up watching Manchester United play a lot of times on the television, first with my dad and then with my sons, so I can't be sure whether or not I ever heard their names before.

There was another time when I knew that someone was messing about with me. At first I could see figures fluttering around me, which could have been the nurses or doctors. Then the bright light was back, and when I stared into the light I could see mum and Tony's dad standing in it again.

While they were standing in the bright light, mum and Tony's dad kept saying, "Come with us. Come with us. You'll only have pain and suffering if you don't come with us. You'll be best coming with us."

Seeing my mum and Tony's dad standing in a bright light and urging me to go with them was something that happened now and again, and every time it happened I just 'knew' that I couldn't do what they said. I had the kids to think of and there were lots of things I still had to do including learning to walk again.

I was completely paralysed when the Physios first started coming twice a day to work me, so all they could do at first was turn me and move my limbs about. Then one day when my 'Named Nurse', Eileen and someone else were washing me, Eileen told me to try and do it for myself. First she brought my right arm over to my left shoulder, holding the cloth in place for me. Then they used my own hand to wash me and they only had to do that a few times before I started doing it for myself.

Somehow my brain must have 'clicked in' and it remembered how to do it, but I could only wash as far as I could reach without having to lean forward. If I'd leant forward to do my legs I would have fallen over, so it was Eileen or whoever else was helping her who washed my legs for me.

The best thing about washing myself was that it started other things going on like getting back some of the use in my right arm and my right leg, and then they gave me exercises for learning how to sit up by myself.

The exercises started off with me being laid out flat. Then I'd have to get my back up and then I'd have to pin my bottom cheeks together, go forward and push myself up keeping my cheeks tight all the time and I did that every chance I got, even though there wasn't a time when I wasn't worn out, and everything took an unbelievable effort.

I'd like to explain how bad the horrible tiredness feels like after you've had a stroke, but there isn't a way to explain it. The only way you can understand is by going through it yourself, and I hope that's something that never happens to you.

All I can say is that the horrible tiredness makes everything you try to do take more effort than you can imagine, but I just couldn't give in to it, and forcing myself through all the exercises the Physios gave me helped me in loads of little stages to work my way up to being able to sit up all by myself.

Once I'd fought my way to sitting up by myself they got me sitting in a chair, but I couldn't keep myself upright. I did try sitting in a normal chair while they fed me with my meals, but I'd just slide out of the chair and under the bedside table knocking the food all over the place, so they got me a special chair that looked like something out of science fiction.

The chair had a belt that went round my waist and another one that went round the top of my chest. There was a headrest at the back of it and that was a Godsend, because then I could get out of bed and sit up by myself while Eileen was feeding me, which someone always had to do because I kept missing my mouth if I tried feeding myself.

Being able to sit out of bed without sliding out of the chair gave me even more determination to keep doing all of the exercises the Physios had given me, even though everything I did really wore me out. But I wasn't too wore out not to be shocked by the state of the clothes that Tony and his mum had brought me in to wear.

The dressing gown, the slippers, the nightdresses and the underwear they'd bought in for me were things that only an old granny would wear, and if it hadn't been for Tony's sister Mary bringing me in some decent nightwear I would have spent all my time in hospital looking like an old woman, which I think is what Tony wanted.

Knowing Tony the way I do and looking back on it all, I think the old granny clothes he'd got me were his way of trying to make me feel so old and so much like an invalid that I'd believe I was completely dependent on him.

As well as the old granny clothes he'd bought me, Tony had also told me that I'd been in my coma for three months, but I couldn't have been because I remember Eileen putting one of those little Christmas trees on my locker.

I also remember helping Eileen to decorate the Ward's Christmas tree. There is no doubt in my mind that Eileen had been handing me the decorations for me to hang wherever I could reach on the Christmas tree.

My aneurysm had burst in the beginning of November, and if I were hanging up Christmas decorations I couldn't have spent three months in a coma, and I think that was just another one of loads of things that Tony would say and do to make me think and feel I was 'brain-damaged-stupid'.

I think Tony's sly mind thought that if he'd got

away with convincing me that I was 'brain-damaged-stupid' he could have done and said anything he liked to me without me being able to argue over anything. But if that was his sly plan it was never going to work, because every time I was awake I would be fighting to do the exercises the Physios had given me, and bit-by-bit I was learning to stand all by myself.

Chapter Twelve

Every time anyone told me I was going to be laid flat on my back in bed for the rest of my life I'd always told them I'd made up my mind I was going to bloody well prove them all wrong, and every time the nurses had cheered me on with "Good! Good! Good for you!"

And then as soon as I was up to it they began taking me down to the gym, twice a day. First they'd help me get changed into a pair of shorts before taking me out into the main gym, where the Physios had pulled two raised up beds together side by side with a space between them in case I needed something to lean on while they were teaching me how to stand and walk again.

They'd started me off with simple things like learning to move my legs on my own and when I could do that for myself, they got me to put one foot in front of the other, moving forward all the time.

There were always two physios at the front of me and one at the back just to make sure I didn't fall, and every time we did those walking exercises I would do a little bit more until I could get to the far end of the beds. And once I could do that the physios would hold onto me while they got me to turn around and it was always 'Go! Go! Go!' with me.

I won't pretend I wasn't frightened of falling, and a lot of the time I was shaking and trembling but there was never a time that I didn't want to give it my 'best shot', which must have sometimes worried the Physios who were always asking me "Are you sure you're not too tired?"

Whenever they'd ask me if I was tired I'd always tell them I wasn't, and to keep on going. If you're going to give something you're best shot, you've always got something to prove, and then you've 'got' to do it.

There were probably loads of times I didn't manage to do it, but I always tried my hardest with everything they gave me to do in the Gym as well as all the exercises I did for myself on the Ward, and even if I didn't manage to do it I would always keep on trying and always keep on smiling. That's probably why the nurses and physios always made me their 'Star Patient' and whenever the other Physio 'regulars' saw me coming into the Gym they used to shout out, "Oh! Smiler's here!"

What with all the nurses and physios making me their 'Star Patient', as well as the other regulars cheering me on in the Gym, and my constant exercising I went from learning to sit up on my own to being able to stand and transfer myself by the time Christmas was over. And what a Christmas I had on that Ward!

For a quite a while I'd been buying those really big bars of chocolate for everyone that was helping me, and as soon as they were letting me go into the kitchen on my own I began making the nurses and doctors cups of tea or coffee whenever they came onto the Ward.

When I told that to my writing helper they couldn't work out how I managed to make cups of tea and coffee with only the one good arm and only the one good leg to help me. So I'm going to explain it now, in the same way I explained it to my writing helper.

Being able to stand up and transfer by myself meant I could reach the cups on my own. Then I'd put the cup on top of the kitchen work surface where I'd put what I needed into the cup before pushing it under the tap on the Urn with the boiling water in it. Then all I had to do was turn on the tap.

When the tea or coffee was ready I'd sit myself back in my wheelchair and using my right leg and my right arm I'd turn the wheelchair around. When I'd managed to get it turned around I'd pick up the cup in my right hand and hold it while I shuffled the wheelchair over to the person who needed the drink, using my right leg to pull myself along.

Most of the time the person I was making the drink for would take it off me as soon as I'd picked up the cup and turned around. That's how I used to make teas and coffees for the doctors and nurses on Ward 5.

While I was in the kitchen I was having a proper drink of the brandy or the whiskey that people had brought in for the staff's Christmas Celebrations, and I wasn't depriving the staff because I always bought them back as much and more than I drank.

Now I have to say that all of the nurses, physios and doctors who came onto that Ward weren't just rules and uniforms. They were 'real' people with whom I had so much fun and so many good times I think I was getting away with murder. But there was one night when we came really close to getting ourselves into serious trouble.

I was having a proper drink in the kitchen with some of the staff who were only on teas and coffees, and I don't remember who started it off but we all got onto saying how we should go out for a 'jama' (pyjama) party.

They said that as I was already wearing my 'jamas' they should come in wearing theirs. Then all they would have to do was put me in my wheelchair and wheel me round all the pubs, and we were right in the middle of planning our 'pub crawl' when someone rang the bell for the nurses.

It was one of the women nearest the kitchen who rang the bell to complain that she couldn't sleep because of the racket we were making. So you can see that I had a lot of fun and I'm sure it was all the fun I had with the Ward doctors, nurses and physios that helped me keep going, especially when I was worn out with all the constant exercising I was forcing myself to do.

Now this is where I have to say that the more you enjoy the life you have the more you have to look forward to. And the more you have to look forward to the more you find it in yourself to fight and try even harder.

Having loads of fun on Ward 5 is what kept me fighting and I'm going to take this chance to thank all of the doctors, nurses and Physios who helped me get better by letting me have a laugh and loads of fun with them, which I really needed when I started going home at the weekends.

Tony's mother had moved into the house to do the cooking and housework, and the first weekend they took me through the back door into the kitchen I almost died of shock because even with my tunnel vision I could see that all of the kitchen walls were as brown as a berry.

Tony's mum had never opened the windows while she was cooking and smoking her cigarettes, and where the steam from the cooking had mixed with the nicotine on the walls it had all run down in long brown streaks. It looked awful but there was nothing I could do or say because Tony's only interest was in trying to brainwash me again.

The way he'd started out with trying to convince me I was brain-damaged-stupid was by making out that most of the time I didn't know what I was doing. There was nothing he did or said that was big enough to catch him out, but there were lots of little things he'd say or do to make me doubt myself like telling me I'd done or said this and that when I knew that I hadn't. Or if something weren't where it should have been, Tony would say that I was the one who had it last, so it must have been me who had put it somewhere it shouldn't have been.

Deep down I always knew I hadn't done anything Tony accused me of doing, but he never let up and his constant going on was beginning to make me think there might be something wrong with my brain, which I might have ended up believing if it wasn't for my Named Nurse, Eileen.

At the Weekends when I was home from Friday to Sunday night, there was no one for me to talk to about my brain because Tony wouldn't let me go into the hall and that was where we had our phone. He said the reason I wasn't allowed there was because if someone rang I was too slow to get to the phone in time, which I couldn't understand.

Everyone who knew me knew that I'd been disabled by a stroke, and Tony must have known that even if I didn't get to the phone in time for their first call they'd have called me back again. Another thing I couldn't understand was why none of my family and friends ever wanted to come and see me.

What I didn't know was that Tony had banned my eldest son from coming to see me, and if any of my friends came to visit Tony would tell them I was sleeping and I was too tired out to be disturbed. But this wouldn't have stopped him from waking me up if there was something he wanted to know from me, so what was the difference?

If he wasn't keeping me isolated until he'd convinced me there was something wrong with my brain then he would have woken me up and let me talk to my visitors, which is something I might have never realised if I hadn't managed to get to the phone one day when Tony went out.

I'd been given a perching stool and it didn't take me long to work out that if I half-stood, like I did in the kitchen on the Ward, I could pull the stool forward with my right hand and then sit down and then stand up again while I pulled the chair forward with my right hand again.

That way I could get myself into the hallway to use the phone which Tony never realised, and when I was sure he was properly out of the way that day, I shuffled myself into the hall and rang my Named Nurse, Eileen to ask her what was going wrong with my brain. She told me there was nothing at all wrong with it.

Eileen said my brain was sound and it was Tony that was the problem. She said that when they'd first met Tony they all thought he was really nice and a really good husband to me. But then he'd tried to 'chat the nurses up', which put them right off him, and none of the nurses liked or trusted Tony at all

Hearing that and knowing I could always look to Eileen and the other nurses for the real truth put my mind at rest, which gave me a lot more of the strength I needed for dealing with Tony and the horrible ways he was using to make me believe I was brain-damaged-stupid. In fact he was the one who was stupid because he and his sister Tricia were making a right mess out of running the Café.

After I'd first 'come round' enough from the stroke to understand what was going on, Tony and his mother had told me I'd been replaced at the Café with Tony's sister Tricia, whom I knew was such a terrible cook she couldn't even boil an egg without bursting it.

With Tricia's terrible cooking they were lucky if they were making £20.00 a week, which wasn't enough to cover the overheads or to buy enough food to keep a Café going for a full week. They were getting overdraft after overdraft just to keep the Café going. And every time Tony came to visit me in the hospital, during the week, he would spend all the time 'nattering' me about the mess they were in.

At first it was more about what do next for the Café, or with his sister Tricia having bought too much of something and what was he going to do? It was always stupid things like the time Tricia bought too much cheese and they didn't know what to do. So I had to tell him to cut the cheese into blocks and freeze them all until they needed another block.

With that out of the way Tony would move on to moaning about how much work he had to do. He would just go on and on about how many places he had to go and how many things he had to do, and how having to spend so much of his time visiting me was making it difficult for him.

None of this could have been happening the way Tony was moaning because my eldest son Mark had gone to live at his girlfriend's parent's house and there was nothing Tony had to do for him.

Our youngest son Philip was being taken to school and brought back by a friend of mine called Dot who lived across the road from us.

Tony's mum was doing all of the cooking and neither of them were doing any proper housework, so all Tony had to do at home was eat, sleep, watch the 'telly' and moan.

The Café was only open for six hours a day (8 a.m. to 2 p.m.) and Tony had his sister to do all the cooking and cleaning for him, and with me going home every Friday to Sunday evening, it was obvious that Tony didn't really have much to do at all.

Once I'd weighed everything up, I knew Tony was only trying to make me feel guilty and his moaning shouldn't have got to me but by the time the month of March came round I was so sick of his constant 'guilt trips' that I asked them to give me an early discharge from the hospital- which they didn't really want to do.

What they really wanted to do was keep me on Ward 5 until they thought I was well enough and strong enough to be able to go home for good. Only they didn't have to put up with Tony, and I kept on and on at them until I managed to talk them into letting me go home for good somewhere between the beginning of March and the start of April.

Having to say goodbye to the staff on Ward 5 was a really emotional experience for all of us. The young doctor who'd diagnosed me when I'd arrived in Casualty had already left the BRI a few months after I'd come back from Pinderfields, and when he'd come to say his goodbyes to the all staff on Ward 5 I'd thanked him for saving my life.

When he'd told me he was only doing his job, I'd told him that wasn't right, and that if it hadn't been for him working out what could have been wrong with me I would have been dead, and it was he who'd saved my life that night.

Telling the young doctor the truth about what he'd done for me left him in tears, and there were a lot more tears when it was my turn to leave Ward 5 and I'd told all the staff how grateful I was and how sad I was to be leaving them. Then Eileen took me down in my wheelchair and helped me get into Tony's car.

When I got home, the first and only thing I wanted to do was to go and lie down in my bed which Tony had brought down to the Dining Room when I first started going home at the weekends. But before I could get into my bed and go to sleep, I had to clear the dust off the bed as well as getting the sheets changed, which I know from the way a woman knows that they hadn't been changed from the last weekend I'd been at home.

I also knew from past weekends that everything in my Dining Room was caked in dust and I would have to clean everything up myself, once I'd had a rest and got some of my strength back. But I wasn't going to wait to change the sheets.

Having to change the sheets made me realise there was so much I was going to have to do if I wanted a home fit for me and my youngest to live in, but first I needed a lot of sleep, and every time I'd lie down for a rest or if I was going off to sleep, I would see the bright light with mum and Tony's dad in it. They were still telling me "You're going to be going through a lot of pain and trouble. You'd be best coming off with us. Come here! Come here!"

And maybe I should have 'gone' with them because I'd only got home on the Friday, and early the following Monday morning Tony woke me to tell me that Tricia had rung him to say that she wasn't going in to work. It was myself who had to work in the Café, and I'd have to start that morning.

Chapter Thirteen

The two years following my early discharge from the BRI were such a non-stop physical and emotional 'Roller Coaster Ride' that I can't give an exact time and date to everything that happened. What I can say is what did happen and the way it happened within a few weeks of it happening, and I'm going to start with the Monday morning Tony took me to work at the Café.

I had tunnel vision in my right eye and I was almost blind in the left when I went into the Café for the first time since my burst aneurysm, but I couldn't miss the big sink full of dirty plates, cups, cutlery, cooking utensils and pans all sitting in horrible looking cold, greasy water that I didn't even want to look at, never mind touch. But you can't run a Café without the things that were in that sink, and I didn't have long to work out how I was going to get them clean.

Having only one good hand and one good leg to help me meant I had to find some way of doing the washing up, and in the end I worked out that if I wedged one plate or pan or cooking utensil against the bottom edge of the sink I could scrub my way all round the inside or the outside of whatever it was that needed cleaning. If it weren't clean enough when I checked it on the draining board, I'd start all over again.

Sitting at the Café sink on my perching stool, doing the washing up one-handed, one piece at a time was such slow and tiring work I can't even begin to explain how I felt by the time I'd done it all, and that was only the start of my work.

I still had to prepare all the meat and the 'Veg', and I had to learn new ways of doing that too. We had no machine to peel the potatoes so I got Tony to knock four stainless steel nails through a piece of wood and then I'd stick each potato on the nails while I peeled it, turned it and peeled it, until every potato was done.

Once all the potatoes were peeled, I'd use my right hand to lift my left arm onto the worktop where I'd take one potato at a time and push it up against my left fist, which I used as a 'stop' while I cut the potato into thick scallops. I would then cut these into thick chips unless I wanted them in bigger pieces for roasting.

Carrots got 'topped and tailed' on the chopping board and then I'd put each carrot upright in my left hand. My left arm wasn't working at all, but a little bit of a grip had returned to my left hand and I'd use it to keep the carrot in place. Then I'd use my tummy to pin my left hand with the carrot in it against the work surface.

When I was sure the carrot wasn't going to fly out

of my hand, I'd use the knife in my right hand to peel my way down before cutting it into slices with the knife coming in from the front, and with my right thumb keeping the back of the carrot in place.

Slicing up carrots that way gave me a permanent split in the pad of my right thumb, until I learned how to get the pressure of the knife going through the carrot just right, and then the knife only just touched the pad of my thumb when it went through to the other side of the carrot.

Onions got 'topped and tailed' like the carrots before being chopped in half, peeled and pushed against my left fist for chopping into slices in much the same way I scalloped the potatoes and if I wanted the onion diced, I'd chop the slices up.

As each lot of 'Veg' that needed boiling was ready, I'd put them into a pan. Then I'd put a smaller pan in the sink and fill it up from the tap before transferring the water to the larger pan, which I had to do over and over again with every pan of 'Veg'.

Once each pan of 'Veg' was full enough, I'd get it onto the gas hob by dragging the pan along the worktop. First I'd shuffle along my perching stool to where I could just reach the pan, and then I'd drag it right up to me. By shuffling and dragging my way along the worktop I'd get all the 'Veg' on the Gas Hob.

The roasting pans with the meat or the roasting potatoes got put in the oven the same way I moved the 'Veg', and Tony would put the big roasting pans with the really big joints, or the large Turkeys into the oven for me.

We couldn't risk me getting burnt by a red-hot roasting pan, just in case I dropped it and that would have lost us a lot of money, so Tony would give me a hand with getting them out of the oven.

Everything I did was really slow and tiring at first, but with each week that passed I kept getting faster and faster until I could prepare the food, do the washing up and use my perching stool to get myself round the Café as fast as anyone else.

By the time the second week was up, I'd even worked out that if Tony cracked a load of eggs into a poacher I could do the fried eggs when I needed them without having to keep on calling him over to crack them for me.

The only things I couldn't teach myself to do on my own was to crack eggs, cut the bread rolls in half and butter them. So Tony did the bread rolls and 'his share' of the work while I was preparing all the food and doing all the cooking. If we ran out of something, he'd make an extra trip to the 'Cash and Carry', but that wasn't very often.

After the first week was over I usually knew what we would need for our next week and I'd go to the 'Cash and Carry' with Tony because I couldn't really trust him not to get 'crap'; which he would have done if I'd let him go on his own.

Before he met me, Tony had never eaten meat in his life. The only meat his mother ever bought was beef brisket which can be tough, stringy, fatty and full of gristle if you don't know what joint to pick or how to cook it properly. And I'm not being unkind when I say that Tony's mother didn't have a clue how to tell a good joint from a bad one, or how to cook the one she'd bought.

Tony's mother was such a terrible cook that in the first week and a half she stayed on at our house, we all used to wait until her back was turned to throw her food into the bin without eating any of it, and it's a good job she only stayed with us until she knew she wasn't wanted, which was about a week and a half.

Once Tony's mother was gone, my youngest didn't have to rely on his school dinners any more and we could stop having to fill ourselves up on bacon sandwiches at the Café, until I'd eaten so many bacon sandwiches that I used to make myself mushroom sandwiches just for a change.

Now that I mention mushrooms, I've just remembered another thing I didn't do in the Café and that was to slice up the mushrooms. Not because I couldn't do it, but because Tony said I couldn't cut them thin enough and he'd banned me from slicing mushrooms.

Being banned from slicing mushrooms didn't help me much with my workload because on top of all the work I had to do for the Café, Tony's mum had left my house in such a state there was loads to do before I could make the house into a half-decent home for me and my son.

As for the Café being fit for our customers, Tricia had done so little cleaning that the brand new units, cupboards and worktops were still full of sawdust from the time they'd been fitted, and it did take me quite a while to clean everything up, but within a few weeks the Café was looking like somewhere you'd want to eat.

At this point my writing helper wanted to know what Tony was doing while I was doing so much of the work for the Café. That was one question I never saw coming and it really took me by surprise. It was something I'd never, ever thought about, and the truth is that after a lot of thinking I don't really remember Tony doing much work at all.

Though I do want to be fair and tell it exactly how it was, I have thought about it again and the only things I can really remember Tony ever doing for the Café was cracking the eggs, cutting the bread rolls in half, buttering the bread rolls, slicing mushrooms, making sandwiches, putting the really heavy roasting pans in the oven, taking the red-hot roasting pans out of the oven, going to the cash and carry, and serving the orders.

The only time I did have any help in the first weeks at the Café was when Tony's sister, Tricia came back to work on the Wednesday after I started working there, but that was only for the one day and she never showed up again.

That meant there was never a day I didn't leave the Café worn out, but I couldn't give in to being tired out because when I got home I still had our 'tea' to get ready.

Most evenings I'd only have to put the potatoes and the 'Veg' on to cook, because I'd peeled our potatoes, prepared our 'Veg' and left them in cold water the night before ready to just rinse off and put on to cook.

Before I left for the Café every morning, I'd put the meat in the oven on a very low setting to slow cook until we got home. That way it never took long to get our 'tea' ready and once we'd all finished our 'tea' I'd have the clearing up and washing up to do.

When all of that was done I'd be so worn out I'd have to lie down and take a rest in my bed before I started getting us ready for the next day at the Café. This involved cutting the rind off of the bacon, washing and slicing the cucumbers, grating all the cheese and whatever else I could do in advance which included getting our 'tea' ready for cooking the following evening.

Even then my work wasn't done because Tony's mum had broken my washing machine while I was in the hospital so I had to wash the towels and tea towels from the Café by hand in the sink.

The only laundry I couldn't do by hand was the big stuff like the sheets. Things like that had to be taken to the Laundrette and then I'd had to teach myself how to do the ironing, or Tony would never have had his smart pants, white shirt and white overall looking good enough for serving our customers in our Café, as well as for going to the 'Cash and Carry'.

I was doing so much work and I was so tired all the time that I don't remember exactly when the horrible headaches started, but I do remember them getting so bad I told Mr Towns when I went to see him for one of my regular checkups.

Mr Towns sent me for a CT Scan and when the results came back he told me it was only some fluid left over from when they'd had to drill the holes in my head. He told me not to worry, but I do wonder what he would have said if he'd known how much I was having to do, though I did tell my new physios at St Lukes how much work I was doing.

Before I'd left the BRI I'd been booked in for twice weekly afternoon sessions of physiotherapy at St Lukes Hospital, and the physios weren't used to working with someone like me, so they were all amazed when they first found out I was working in the Café. My new physios couldn't understand how I was doing what I said I was doing, so I showed them.

They'd never seen anything like it before and that's why I can understand why someone reading my story could find it hard to get their head around how I was managing to do all the work that I say I was doing.

But being amazed and being shown what I had taught myself to do didn't mean the physios were happy with me, or with what I was doing and they told me that having been discharged so soon after a burst aneurysm I shouldn't be doing so much work. They wanted me to cut right back on what I was doing until I'd built up my strength and energy.

It would have been nice if I could have done what the physios wanted me to do, but Tony and Tricia had made such a bad job of running the Café that it was close to bankrupt, and I had no other choice but to carry on the way I was going.

If I didn't keep doing what I was doing we would have lost everything we owned, and Tony's mum would have lost her home as well. So I just had to keep working and as soon as we had enough customers for the Sandwich side of the business I began doing baked potatoes, which I baked while I was doing the other preparation work at night, and then I only had to heat them up in the microwave at the Café.

Putting on baked potatoes went so well that after my first month in the Café our business had picked up to where I started making things like Shepherd's Pie for dinner times, and when that took off I went on to doing 'puds' (puddings) as well.

Then Tony's sister Mary started making us things like Curries, Chilli Con Carne, and Lasagne which helped me out so much I could begin making my house a fit place for me and my son to live in, and I started off with cleaning up my kitchen.

The brown-streaked mess Tony's mum had made on all the walls in my kitchen had got on my nerves so bad I 'had' to get them clean. I did this by first moving the kitchen table to where I wanted to start the cleaning and then I'd get myself onto the table from where I'd use Sugar Soap and water to scrub down the parts of the wall that I could reach.

Being up on top of the kitchen table scared me to death, and I'm not going to bore you by going on and on about my disabilities or how tired I was, or how hard it was to get myself up on top of the table. The only important thing is that bit-by-bit I worked my way around my kitchen walls every chance I got until they were clean enough for me.

Once I'd finished getting my kitchen walls clean enough, I cleaned up the dust from my living and dining rooms before moving on to cleaning the upstairs rooms, which I got to by teaching myself how to go upstairs on my bum one step at a time.

While all that was going on I was still keeping in contact with Eileen. She was such a good friend to me that during my second week at the Café she took me out shopping for a pair of flat shoes that I badly needed for working in the Café, because the only shoes I'd ever worn since I left school were stiletto heels, and the only flat shoes I'd had in all that time were a pair of high-sided trainers I'd got for my Physio sessions.

It was during one of our little chats on the phone that I'd mentioned to Eileen I needed a pair of flat shoes for working in the Café, and she was such a good friend to me that was all it needed for Eileen to come round as soon as she could and take me out shopping.

After that first shopping trip Eileen kept on coming round every couple of weeks to take me out shopping, and what a laugh we always used to have together! There was the time that Eileen was taking me over to meet her mother and she had to stop off at the Supermarket just to pick up a few things her mother wanted.

There wasn't much for Eileen to get for her mother, but she took the time out to help me into my wheelchair and take me round the supermarket with her. This didn't take long and we were doing so much talking and laughing while she was putting the things in the boot of the car I forgot to put the brake on my wheelchair which went rolling off down the car park with me in it shouting, "Eileen! Eileen! Help me! I'm running away!"

Another time in another Supermarket, Eileen left me in one of the aisles while she went back to get something she'd missed. She was only supposed to be gone for a moment or two and she probably wasn't away that long, but I got nervous from being without her and I started shouting at the top of my voice, "Eileen! Eileen! Where are you! You've forgotten all about me!"

I made so much noise with shouting for Eileen that when she came running back, everyone was looking at me like I was daft or something and the pair of us found it all so funny we were nearly wetting ourselves with laughter by the time we got to the checkout.

There were so many funny things that seemed to happen to us in Supermarkets and Car Parks that I can't help laughing when I remember some of the sillier things that always seemed to happen every time we went out somewhere together.

When I look back on those days, I believe it was seeing Eileen every couple of weeks or when she realised I really needed her support that helped me get through everything I had to get through, especially when the Café got so busy we had to bring in a girl to help us out.

Getting someone in to help me might sound nice and caring of Tony, but he didn't hire the extra help I needed until after I'd had to crack him over the head with the heaviest frying pan I could lay my hand on, after he'd told me- "What we need is someone able-bodied in here."

I think that's probably when I got my hatred of the term 'able bodied', and I also think that's probably when Tony first realised I could stand up to him, because after that it wasn't long before he started calling me 'thick, stupid, and dumb' all over again and this time he added 'useless' to the list. This hurt me a lot because I was doing everything while Tony was doing 'naff all', or as little as possible.

Calling me names all over again really hurt, and it got even worse for me when the horrible violence and horrible cruelty he'd shown after my mum died began to creep in, again. Every time I stood up to Tony, or told him he was wrong when he said I'd done this or that, or I'd said this or that when I knew I hadn't he would 'batter' me, whether I was in or out of my wheelchair and he was always sly enough to hit me where no one could see the marks, except for the one time when he'd punched me in the face and it came out in a bruise.

When Tony saw the size of the bruise and how bad it was he pleaded for me not to tell his son that he'd hit me, which I wouldn't have done because I loved my kids and I couldn't have hurt my youngest by letting him know what a horrible bastard his father really was. So it was love for my son and not his dad's pleading that got me to lie when my youngest asked me how I'd got the bruise on my face and I'd told him I'd banged myself on something.

But as bad as it got, I kept finding the strength to keep going until I'd turned the business around, which wasn't easy because Tony had built up a lot of debts and overdrafts while I was in the hospital and having to pay off Tony's debts out of our weekly cash flow, wasn't leaving us with enough for me to keep expanding our business. However, I'd managed to build it up from taking only about £20 to £30 a week, to taking between £100 to £200 a day, six days a week if you counted up to the end of lunchtime on Saturday mornings.

That was good money, but we still needed more for the Cash and Carry as well, and for keeping up with the overheads. You can't run a Café without food, gas and electric, so I fixed up a meeting with our Bank Manager who came over to the Café. I took her through the books and after I'd told her and showed how the business was building up and getting better, I asked her if she thought I'd come out of hospital early not to make a go of it?

Our Bank Manager was just as amazed as the physios had been when they found out about all the work I was doing, and when she saw the amount of money we'd started to take she gave us another overdraft which meant we could hire a girl to help us.

The only trouble with hiring a girl was that the girl Tony chose for the job was so bloody lazy that all she ever wanted to do was stand there looking out of the window. I kept trying to get Tony to say something to her. But he wouldn't say anything, so I gave her the 'bollocking' Tony should have given her and I made her start working for her wages.

Tony wasn't best pleased that I'd 'bollocked' the girl when he didn't have the nerve to do it himself, so he 'battered' me for doing what he should have done. But as far as I was concerned it didn't matter what Tony liked or didn't like or how often he 'battered' me because the business was building up so fast we had to get more equipment.

We'd started out with a big fridge for drinks and salads which was enough for the custom the Café had when Tony and Tricia were running it into the ground, but it wasn't enough for what I'd built up and we had to get ourselves another big fridge for keeping more ready-made salads, buns, pies, and all that sort of thing.

Getting the second big fridge helped a lot and we were doing really well until I started having dizzy spells and fainting 'dos', which my doctor said was down to exhaustion, and when he'd taken my blood pressure he made me go straight into St Lukes Hospital to be treated for serious exhaustion. I don't know how long they wanted to keep me in St Lukes, but after a week of being bored to death I started pestering them to let me out.

The main doctor in charge of the Ward wouldn't let me go home until they got my blood pressure right down, so it was lucky for me there was a really nice young Chinese doctor who came onto the Ward when the main one was off, because I managed to talk him into letting me out early.

That was sometime in September or October of 1991 and being made to go into hospital with really bad exhaustion forced me into facing the truth that I couldn't keep on doing all the work I was doing, and I made up my mind that the Café had to be sold off, even though the whole country had gone into a bad recession. This meant there weren't many people about who wanted to start up in business, but in the six to seven months I'd been working in the Café I'd managed to build it up enough for us to be able to sell it off as a 'going concern'.

That way we never lost any money on what we'd paid for the Café, but no one had kept any kind of accounts before I started working there so I never got to know how much of a debt we'd been put in with all of Tony's overdrafts, or if he'd borrowed from anyone else.

What I do know is that the money we did get from the sale couldn't have been enough to pay off all of Tony's debts, because in the end his mother had to sell her house to pay off the mortgage she'd taken out for her and her son. This wasn't my fault because I'd worked myself into exhaustion in a recession just to get the Café from being a loss making business to being a 'going concern'.

You would have thought that saving us from going bankrupt would have made Tony happy, but that wasn't the way he saw it, and from the day the Café went up for sale he never stopped blaming me for having to sell it off.

Instead of thanking me for what I'd done and how much work I'd put into the business, he was forever going on and on at me with saying it was my fault he'd lost his business, and that if it weren't for me he would still have a business.

Blaming me for having to sell the Café off along

with all the other horrible things Tony was doing to me built up to where I felt so bad that when my 40th Birthday came around, I did my best to kill myself.

Chapter Fourteen

We needed to get some money coming into the house while the Café was up for sale and with G.T. Smith's autumn audit being due I got in touch with Carol who also thought it was worth looking into even though we didn't know if they'd given the job to anyone else - which they hadn't - because a few phone calls later the job was ours and they were ready for us to start.

Tony drove me to Carol's home in Wakefield and from there her husband drove us to G.T. Smith's main offices in Knottingley. Both of the brothers and some of the staff came down to welcome us back. They all knew I'd had a bad stroke and that Carol would be taking me round in a wheelchair, so they'd set aside an office for us to work from.

One of the brothers took us to see our new office, and after we'd taken a good look round he asked us if there was anything else that we needed. When we said there wasn't, he told us they'd given us our own phone and all we had to do was to call them if ever we did need anything else. Then every day one of the brothers or some of the girls would come to our office to ask us how we were getting on and see if we needed anything.

Even with all the help they wanted to give us, the audit was a lot harder and slower at first than I'd thought it was going to be because my aneurysm had given me tunnel vision in my right eye and all I could see with my left eye was a 'black wall' running out from the middle of my face. The 'black wall' ended not far from my face in a weird sort of haze.

Trying to work with figures through a 'black wall' and a weird haze was so irritating that I had to put some tape over the left lens of my glasses and that made looking at figures a lot easier for me, but it didn't help me with entering the figures into my Comptometer which really needed both hands for putting in things like the £ signs, so I had to learn how to do it all with just one hand.

Both problems kept making my work really slow and awkward at first, but I kept at it and the more I kept at it the quicker I got though I was never going to be as fast as I'd been with both hands. I didn't mind this because working at G.T. Smith's was like a big breath of fresh air after the Café.

All the other girls couldn't have been any nicer to us and there was always time for a laugh and a joke with them. And when I told them how I'd hit Tony over the head with the heaviest frying pan we had in the Café they all fell about laughing.

Working with so many nice, friendly and helpful people along with getting the audit done in time gave my confidence such a big boost that I wanted to keep on going with the business, but I must have made Tony so jealous of me being able to get back into business without him the dickhead refused to drive me over to Carol's any more.

Not being able to get to Carol's left me stuck at home with so much time on my hands that my mind went back to wondering about my eldest son and why he'd never come to visit me when I first came home from the BRI, or why he didn't come round more often now that the Café was gone and I was nearly always at home.

Another thing I kept wondering was why he was giving Tony money before he came into the house. Though I had asked Tony why he was taking the money off my son, all I could ever got out of him was that my son 'wanted to pay us Board because he knew our money situation'.

I knew that wasn't the truth when he said it but with Tony always hovering around when anyone came to see me I'd never been able to ask my eldest son. I had no other way of finding out what was really going on because my son, Mark had moved into a flat with his girlfriend and they didn't have a phone.

That meant I just had to keep on wondering until one day my son came round when Tony was out and I took that chance to ask him what was going on between him and Tony. He told me that Tony had told him if he wanted to see me then he would have to pay him

Board, which was so stupid of Tony.

My son didn't need blackmailing to help us out. If we'd told him we were struggling he would have helped us anyway, and what Tony was doing to get money out of my son made me both angry and sad. Just because my eldest son wasn't his son didn't make it right for Tony to be forcing him to pay him money to see his own mum, so as soon as Tony came home I asked him what he thought he was playing at and why was he making my son give him money just to see me.

Of course Tony denied it all like he always did when he was doing something wrong. He said that I didn't know what I was talking about and the only reason my son was giving him 'Board Money' when he wasn't living with us was because he knew our money situation and he just 'wanted to help us out'.

When I refused to accept Tony's 'story' he 'battered' me like he always did when I stood up to him and though he hurt me a lot I think it was Tony who came off the worst, because from then on my son mostly came to see me when he knew Tony was out and Tony must have lost some of the money he would have needed for paying his prostitutes.

I know I've said Tony had gone impotent before I'd had my stroke, but my being badly disabled seemed to have 'cured' him and he'd gone back to raping me even though the stroke had left me with a permanent period. But he wasn't using condoms when he was raping me, so why did me and my youngest son keep seeing packets of Durex on the dashboard of his car?

And another good reason for believing Tony was

going prostituting was that for a long time he'd been going out late at nights when he had no friends of his own, and it wasn't for having affairs because I knew more than enough people that would have known and told me if that was what he was doing.

So what did Tony 'have' to do that was so secret he couldn't tell me, but was so important he 'had' to go out late on the night of my 40th Birthday which should have been the best birthday I'd ever had in my life?

Loads of the people we knew had kept telling us that I should have a really big 'Do' to celebrate being still alive and for me having proved everyone wrong when they said I'd be laid flat on my back in bed, paralysed for the rest of my life. Tony knew that all the talk about me having a really big 'Do' had got me right excited about my birthday, so when he went out and got us enough drink for a really good party I did think I was going to have a 'big day'.

But when my 40th Birthday came round on the 13th of October 1991 there was no going out for a meal and no big party for me. The only ones that Tony invited to celebrate my 40th with me were Ann from my clothes party days and her new husband Ian, the lad from the Ring 'O' Bells pub that Ann married after she'd left and divorced her husband.

I did try and make the best of it, but my big 'Do' wasn't much of a night and it only lasted until Ann and her new husband had to go back to Halifax. Then Tony went out to do his 'prostituting', leaving me to celebrate my 'special' birthday with only a load of drink to keep me company.

149

Being left on my birthday with only a load of drink to keep me company I started thinking about the horrible year Tony had put me through and what a horrible life I had to look forward to with Tony who was still trying to make me believe I was brain-damaged-stupid.

He was trying so hard to convince me I was brain-damaged-stupid by constantly telling me I'd said that or I'd done this when I knew that I hadn't, he ended up torturing his own son with trying to drag him into his arguments against me by shouting at our poor lad, Philip with things like, "She did. Didn't she! Tell her she did! Go on! Tell her she did!"

The lad was quiet, anyway and Tony would always get him so confused that all he could do was sit there looking from one of us to the other, and when that didn't make me back down and say that I had done or said what he claimed I'd done or said, Tony would 'batter' me.

The more I thought about Tony and what he was doing to me the less I wanted to live until I finally got to where I truly believed the only way I was going to get any rest or peace from Tony's, 'battering' raping and tormenting me was to kill myself, so I got all my tablets and started taking some with every drink.

I'd already taken lots of tablets and done lots of drinking when I realised that no one would know why I'd killed myself, so I got a felt tip pen and I started writing everything down on the kitchen walls and the kitchen floor.

There was so much for me to write down that I

can't remember if I started off with Tony's 'battering', raping and tormenting me, or that he'd told me he was 'glad I was the way that I was because I couldn't do anything without him', or that he wouldn't stop going on and on with telling me I was 'thick, dumb, stupid and useless', as well as taunting me with things like, "You walk like a snail! A tortoise or a snail can walk faster than you! It's your fault I lost my business. If it weren't for you I'd still have a business!"

Somewhere in all that writing I told everyone about how I'd nearly killed myself from overwork with sorting out the mess he'd made of the Café and how it was he who had stopped me from having my own business by refusing to take me over to Carol's at Wakefield, even though we needed the money and he wasn't doing anything else at the time.

When I'd finished getting all that down, I wrote about how he'd run over my foot on purpose when I'd tried to stop him from going out late one night to do his 'prostituting', and how he kept saying he was fed up with being a taxi for me, but when I'd wanted a car (automatic) of my own he wouldn't let me get one, because he wasn't having me 'buggering off all over the shop like I used to do'.

By the time I'd 'passed-out' from the tablets and the drink I'd covered the kitchen walls and the kitchen floor with my writing, which no one ever got to read because Tony must have cleaned it all away before he called the ambulance just in case the ambulance crew got to read it.

Cleaning off all that felt tip pen must have taken

Tony ages before he called the ambulance, but he didn't take long enough for me to get what I wanted because they got me to Casualty in time and managed to 'sort me out' enough to put me on a Ward with young girls that had tried to kill themselves as well.

I can't recall the name of the Ward, but I do remember how ashamed I felt when I first saw some of the Ward 5 nurses coming. I was so embarrassed from knowing how they'd put so much of themselves into helping me live again that if I saw them coming onto the Ward I'd hide my head under the sheet or my face behind a book.

But even if my head were under the sheet or behind a book the Ward 5 nurses would always come over and say "Hiya Iris! How are you today!"

None of the Ward 5 nurses would let me hide from them, and Eileen must have been keeping them up-to-date about everything because they all told me how they understood and for me not to be so ashamed of myself, which made me feel a lot better about myself and then I started taking notice of what the young girls on the Ward were all telling the nurses when they were being asked why they'd tried to kill themselves.

Loads of young girls who had tried to kill themselves kept coming onto the Ward and far too many of them were saying the reason they'd tried to kill themselves was because their boyfriend wouldn't talk to them, or their boyfriend had 'left them', and when they were asked how long they'd been with their boyfriend a lot of them were telling the nurses stupid times like one week, or two weeks, or at the most it was something like six weeks.

Hearing all the silly reasons the young girls were giving the nurses, as well as knowing the Ward 5 nurses weren't holding it against me for letting them down kept making me feel so much better about myself. The only thing left to bother me was what my kids were thinking of me and when I asked Tony what the kids' thought about what I'd tried to do to myself he said "Oh! I just told them you had to go in with an Asthma attack."

That's when it really came home to me that none of my problems were down to me or with my stroke and I just lay there looking at Tony and thinking- "It's you that's the problem, and it's you that's got to go".

Then when I got home from the hospital Eileen took me to a woman Solicitor whom she knew and the Solicitor went for Legal Aid to get me a divorce. But this had to go on hold because it wasn't long before I was put back into hospital.

I'd been getting some more physiotherapy at St Lukes and after we'd finished with the walking exercises, my physio had me doing balance exercises on something like a big beach ball. When it came time for the physio to help me off the ball he lost his grip on me, and I went right over on my left side hurting my left ankle when I fell.

The physio was so busy apologising and I was so used to pain that neither of us realised how much damage I'd done to my ankle. So I'd just picked myself up with the help of the physio and hobbled off to get changed.

Over the next couple of weeks my left foot would just swing outwards on its own whenever I walked and my left foot flopped about like it wasn't attached to my leg, and when it got to where the ankle hurt so bad I couldn't take it any more I went to see my doctor, who sent me to see an Orthopaedic Specialist at the BRI.

The Orthopaedic Specialist my doctor sent me to see was one of the very best. His name is Mr Bollen and I was really lucky to get an appointment to see him, but I almost spoiled my luck when I went and called him 'Doctor', because Mr Bollen sounded a little bit sharp when he said, "I'm not Doctor. I'm Mister Bollen!"

When I heard him say that in the way he did I couldn't help myself from going "Ooooh!" in a slightly sarcastic sort of way, and then I said something daft that I can't remember any more, for which I did apologise straight away and I seem to remember Mr Bollen might have had a little bit of a smile.

He must have forgiven me because he sent me for some X-Rays as well as letting me have another appointment. It was then I discovered that the fall had made such a mess of my ankle ligaments I could have lost my foot if he hadn't worked out a brand new way of doing a 'Triple Fusion' operation, which he was going to do for me at Woodlands Orthopaedic Hospital.

Because I'd had such a serious aneurysm followed by strokes, they made me go into Woodlands early for a load of tests to see if I could have the operation, and once I'd passed all the tests Mr Bollen made a great success of the operation. However, when I came round from the anaesthetic there were no proper painkillers on the Ward.

Someone had lost the key to the serious drugs cabinet and the only painkillers they had to give me were paracetamol, which did nothing at all to kill the pain and I spent the rest of the day screaming in agony. The nurses kept coming over to ask me if I was all right but I had to wait for the shift to change before a Staff Nurse or a Sister went down to theatre and got the anaesthetist who gave me an injection.

By that time the pain had got so bad the first injection didn't touch it, and they had to give me another dose which did cut down the pain. From then on they managed to keep it down to where it was bearable, but they made me stay in bed and they wouldn't give me one of those wheelchairs with a piece to keep your leg up and straight out, which meant I couldn't go and talk to anyone, and that was horrible.

I liked to talk and it wasn't just myself who liked to have a chat. All the other women on the Ward kept saying how disgusted they were at the way I wasn't being given the chance to talk to anyone, and in the end I got so sick of having to shout across the Ward that I got myself out of bed and into a normal wheelchair which I pulled across the Ward with my right leg, and I went for a proper chat with the other women.

When the nurses caught me sitting and chatting with my foot up on a stool or a chair they gave me a 'bollocking' before putting me back in my bed. But being in bed and shouting across the Ward wasn't my way of getting better, and as soon as the nurses' backs were turned I was back in a normal wheelchair and off chatting again. I kept on doing this until the nurses must have got so tired of 'bollocking' me and putting me back in my bed they just gave up, and then I spent loads of my time just wandering around the Ward in a wheelchair chatting and having a laugh.

That way I had a lot of fun and a lot of laughs before they sent me home with a 'pot' (plastercast) on my leg, which I had to keep non-weight bearing for ages before I was allowed to start putting 11/2 lbs of weight through the leg, and when I could do that I had to start building up the weight.

The 'pot' they'd put on my leg at Woodlands went all the way to my left knee and then each time I got the weight built up enough they'd change the 'pot' for a smaller one, until the last 'pot' they put on my leg was what they called a 'Rocker Pot'.

When the 'Rocker Pot' was taken off they sent me back to St Lukes for more Physio and while all that was going on with me, Tony and our neighbour's wife had gone from having a chat over the fence to getting very close with each other, even though he'd spent all of our time on Buttershaw saying how ugly she looked.

He used to say she was boring because all she ever talked about was kids, and you couldn't have a proper conversation with her, and he wished she'd stop talking to him.

At one point he was even hiding from her, but I don't suppose talking was on his mind after he 'recovered' from being impotent. And I don't suppose her being ugly was as important as saving money on prostitutes, which he might have been glad to pay if only he'd known how much trouble was going to come out of their affair.

Chapter Fifteen

Before I get on with telling this part of my story I have to answer the recent question why I didn't just leave Tony and there are so many answers it would take a whole book to explain. The first of the biggest reasons I can give you is that the real Iris who could stand up for herself against bigger and harder raised kids had been 'battered' and 'nattered' into hiding, though I didn't know it then.

The second is that one of the two men I'd left had stalked me to the edge of a full nervous breakdown; the other had stalked and battered me out of my money before giving me so much grief I lost my kids. There was no reason for me to believe that Tony wouldn't stalk and 'batter' me or even worse after I left him, if I could because I had no money and nowhere to run after mum went and died on me. Even if I did manage to get a place, how was I going to turn it into a home? With Tony not working there was never a safe time for me to get any of my things out of the house, and with me being so badly disabled along with having a young son to look after are just some of the many reasons I can explain.

Anyway, you would have thought Tony and our next-door neighbour's wife were two dogs on heat the way they were always 'sniffing' round each other. Any time Tony's 'girlfriend' left her house he would say he had to go and get something from the shops and he'd be off up the road behind her, even though the one thing Tony never did was go to the shops.

Any time he left the house his 'girlfriend' would go trotting after him. Then loads of different people started telling me they were always seeing the two of them kissing and groping each other behind the shops and when my writing helper asked me how I felt about the affair, I said that I didn't give a shit and I wouldn't have cared if they were 'at it' night and day as long as Tony left me alone.

What the pair of them didn't realise when they were doing their sneaking about was that I was getting a load of laughs out of watching them trying to fool me, because Tony never knew how fast I could go up and down stairs on my backside even with a 'pot' on, and I wasn't going to show him. So he didn't have a clue about all the times I'd be watching and laughing at them from our upstairs window.

Some of the funniest times I ever got out of Tony came when he knew his 'girlfriend's' husband was going to be out for a while. As soon as he knew the coast was clear he'd go walking up the road as if he had somewhere important to be, and when he thought he was out of my sight he'd double back on himself, and then he'd come creeping down the road to her house never knowing that I would be at our upstairs window nearly wetting myself from laughing at how stupid he looked from the way he was sneaking and hiding his way back to his 'girlfriend's' house.

The honest truth was that until I'd worked out where to go and how to bring up my son without having any money, while I was so badly disabled, I didn't give a damn what they were up to. They could have been doing anything they wanted, anywhere they wanted to do it, whenever they wanted to do it, without having to try and fool me because the only thing I really needed out of it all was for Tony to stop his 'battering' and tormenting me, which he wouldn't. Then one day he pushed me too far.

He'd been going on and on at me over the colour of the onions I'd given him with his 'tea' and he just wouldn't stop complaining that they hadn't been brown enough. In the end I got so sick of it all I shouted, "For God's Sake! Does it matter? They're only onions! They were cooked! They just weren't brown!"

That was all it took to set Tony off, and he started to hit me so I hit him that hard over the head with my mum's colander I put a big dent in it, which made him go off to the living room and start drinking lagers. I don't know if it had anything to do with it being his head that had dented my mum's colander, or if it was something else that was going on with me, but whatever it was I felt I just 'had' to kill him.

161

I waited until I could hear by his breathing that he'd drunk himself to sleep. Then I picked up my big kitchen knife, stuffed it under my jumper and went into the living room where Tony was lying on the couch with his eyes closed. When I was sure he wasn't about to wake up I pulled the knife out from under my jumper and raised it as high as I could for the extra force I could get behind the knife when I stabbed it into his chest.

But just as I was about to bring the knife down there was a load of knocking at our back door. It was the lady from over the road who used to help me with doing things like getting the 'tea' ready. She was knocking and shouting, "Hiya Iris. Are you all right? It's only me. Are you coming to let me in?"

Her knocking and shouting was so loud I couldn't take my chance to stab Tony in the chest, and I was in such a hurry to hide the knife back under my jumper I almost sliced myself in two. But I did manage to get it hid without cutting myself open and then I went to let her in. Once she was in the house she stayed so long that by the time she went I'd thought about what it would do to our son when he found out that I'd killed his dad, and I put the knife away.

In those days there were lots of really bad times but don't get me wrong, just because Tony wouldn't stop 'nattering', taunting and 'battering' me doesn't mean I never had any good times, because I was still going out and having a laugh with Eileen, who'd started taking me to nurses' and family 'dos', with her.

Tony used to give us a lift there and back, but he

wasn't invited to most of the 'dos' which I don't think he minded because none of the nurses liked him for the way he'd tried to 'chat them up' while I was on Ward 5. They always froze him out in a way that only a load of nurses can when they really don't like you at all.

One big 'do' that Tony did get invited to was 'J' (Dr J Wright) and his Staff Nurse Sian's wedding reception at a big hotel in Bingley. All the nurses were looking out for me so I ended up having a brilliant time, laughing and joking with them.

We were all falling about with laughing when some of the nurses said it was my 'fault' that 'J' and Sian got married because no one on Ward 5 had ever seen a case like mine before I arrived on the Ward, so 'J' and Sian had been forced to work so close together they'd 'got stuck' together!

There were so many things for us to remember with a whole lot of laughing, but I also wanted a dance. I wasn't wearing my 'Rocker Pot' any more and the first chance I got I had myself a slow dance with 'J'. We were mostly rocking and swaying to the music and at the end of our dance 'J' said to me, "You know I could get struck off for dancing with a patient!"

That was the best night I'd had in years, and this was followed by a whole week spent with Ann and her husband in Whitby. They'd moved to Whitby when they'd bought themselves a Guesthouse that hadn't worked out for them. So they'd sold it and bought themselves a house that was close to the beach.

Tony drove me to Whitby but he didn't stop with me. He just dropped me off and drove himself back to his 'girlfriend' in Bradford leaving me to have a brilliant week on my own with Ann and Ian. When I got home to Bradford, Tony gave me one of the best shocks of my life when he told me I could have a car of my own.

I don't know and I never asked why he changed his mind about me having a car. I just went off and got all the letters and things I needed from the doctors saying I was fit to drive. Then I got myself a Ford Focus Automatic, 'hatchback' and it didn't take me long to get used to driving again.

Being able to drive my own car whenever I wanted meant I was 'free' to go wherever I wanted, and one of the first places I went to was the Ring 'o' Bells pub in Halifax where I'd stayed really good friends with my Company Director and where I still knew loads of people from before I'd had my stroke.

I always used to sit at the corner of the bar and there was always someone I could count on to help me, like whenever I wanted to go to the toilet a lad called Mark used to pick me up, put me over his shoulder and carry me over to the 'Ladies'. He would put me down outside the door and hold it open while I hobbled inside. When I'd finished I used to shout for Mark, who'd then come back for me, hold the door open, pick me up, put me over his shoulder and carry me back to the bar with everyone in fits of laughter.

Saturday nights were always good nights in the Ring 'o' Bells and it was the best night for me to go there. It was the one night of the week I could count on Tony taking his 'girlfriend' into Bradford for a night out, and I could count on the pair of them spending the rest of the night together.

What I didn't know at the time about their Saturday nights sleeping together was that his mum was letting them sleep at her house. All I knew was that with him being gone all night every Saturday night, I could stay out as late as I wanted without coming home to a load of 'nattering'.

And it wasn't just Saturday nights that I went to the Ring 'o' Bells. There were loads of other times like the night Tony had been 'battering' me for something and when he'd finished with his hitting he'd gone into the Living Room where I left him drinking his lagers while I went upstairs, got washed, got changed, got some money out of his pocket and 'buggered off' to Ring 'o' Bells.

I got even more time for myself after Tony's 'girlfriend's' husband Reg got sent to prison for Threatening Behaviour'. The way I heard the story was that Reg had gone down to the Tesco Supermarket on Halifax Road where he'd got the 'Jack' from the boot of the car, and when he got back in the car he sat holding the 'Jack' like a gun and pointing it at people as they walked past him in the car park like he was going to shoot them.

It was only a Car Jack but Reg was the only one who knew what it was and he scared enough people for them to phone and tell the police that a man in Tesco's car park had threatened them with a gun. The police took the phone call so serious they sent loads of police to Tesco where they surrounded Reg in his car. From what I heard they even had a helicopter hovering overhead.

When Reg was taken to court he was sent to prison for 'Using Threatening Behaviour', and when we went to visit him Tony took Reg's wife with us. Before we left the prison Tony promised Reg that we were going to 'look after his wife, while he was inside'. What Tony never told Reg was 'how' he was going to look after his wife or how well he was going to be doing it, because as soon as Reg was safely out of the way in jail they started spending loads of nights together.

Now I can't be sure any more, but I think it was somewhere round the June or July of 1993 that Reg was sent to prison. I think it was then because every time Tony went off to meet his 'girlfriend' he would always be singing his own version of the song 'River of Dreams' by Billy Joel which came out sometime in 1993 if I remember it right.

Tony's version of the song went something like; "I go walking in the night, to my river of dreams where I can finally find what I've been looking for." And if he'd finally found what he was looking for you would have thought he'd have been happy to leave me alone, but for some reason that I never understood, Tony tried to kill me.

At the time, Ann and her husband had sold their house in Whitby and moved back to Halifax. We'd helped them to move and when they'd settled into their new home we all went for a night out, and at the end of the night they invited us back to their house for a coffee and a chat.

Myself and Tony had set off to their house first and

we were there before them, but were waiting for such a long time that we started to wonder if something had happened, like maybe they'd broken down, so I got out the car to wait at the house while Tony went back to look for them.

The road that Ann and her husband lived on was a really long road and was more than wide enough for Tony to turn round where we were. But instead of just turning and driving off, Tony went right to the end of the road before he turned and then waited until I was crossing before he put his foot down and drove the car straight at me.

I could only walk slowly and he was driving so fast that he couldn't have stopped or gone round me in time, so someone was looking out for me that night because I somehow managed to get out of Tony's way in time, and my friend's son came running out to help me up the step. He'd been stood at his bedroom window watching it all as it happened, and he said that Tony had definitely tried to kill me.

The only thing that I don't know about that night is 'why' Tony tried to kill me. I didn't care what he did with his 'girlfriend'. I'd never tried to stop them from doing anything they wanted to do. I had my own car and he didn't have to spend any of his 'girlfriend-time' driving me all over the place. Reg was in jail and Tony could have stopped all day and night in bed with Reg's wife. And on top of all that freedom, Tony knew I was going back into hospital for a second operation on my ankle.

Mr Bollen had been sending me for regular X-rays

which had shown there wasn't enough bone, or good enough quality bone on the inside of the left ankle for the screws that were holding everything in place, and he wanted to put some bone marrow in the ankle to help it heal.

Having another operation on my ankle was all right with me, but I didn't want to go back to Woodlands and when I'd told Mr Bollen how I felt about Woodlands he'd agreed to do my operation at the BRI, where they booked me in to have it done on my birthday!

The morphine pump helped to keep the pain down until I didn't need it any more, and then I finally got discharged with another 'pot' on my left leg. The pot went all the way up to my left knee and my left leg was still non-weight bearing when Reg got out of prison, which must have been sometime near the early part of November 1993.

What with Reg being released from prison you would have thought Tony and his 'girlfriend' would have got a lot more careful with what they were doing. But they just carried on the same way and I don't know what kind of an excuse she could have been giving Reg to cover herself for spending whole nights sleeping with Tony.

Whatever she was telling Reg, the pair of them must have thought they were getting away with it because there was nothing to show that he knew what they were up to when he invited us round for a drink to celebrate his being out of prison. The first time any of us found out that he knew what they were up to was when he suddenly turned on me and said, "Do you know these two are having an affair?"

The words were only just out of his mouth when Reg grabbed his wife to 'batter' her and Tony just stood there without making a move to help her. It's a good job for both of them that she managed to break free and bugger off because Tony would have let Reg kill her.

Reg should have turned on Tony when his wife got away, but he turned on me instead and as soon as Reg's back was turned on him Tony buggered off leaving me there on my own with Reg going on and on at me about the affair. When I tried to leave Reg wouldn't let me out of the house.

I couldn't do much to defend myself with only the one good arm and a 'pot' on a non-weight bearing leg to help me, so I did the only thing I could by trying to talk my way out of it with Reg going on at me like a lunatic and even though I was frightened for my life, I kept trying to talk my way out of getting 'battered' by him.

When I did finally manage to talk my way out of Reg's house, I found that dickhead Tony hiding behind some conifers we had at the end of our right long garden. As I was hobbling my way back to our house, he was peeping out from behind the conifers and he was trying to keep his voice down while he was calling out, "He ain't there is he? He ain't there then? He can't find me? Can he?"

I was so totally disgusted with Tony for the way he was hiding from Reg and for the way he'd run off without trying to protect his 'girlfriend', and for leaving his disabled wife with a lunatic that I just hobbled into the house, leaving him hiding behind the conifers looking stupid.

When Tony wouldn't come into the house, I left him hiding behind our conifers and if he thought getting away from Reg that night was going to be the end of it, then he couldn't have been more wrong in his head because Reg was only just getting started.

Chapter 16

Our youngest son was playing outside, Tony was in the kitchen with me, and I was just sitting at the table when we heard this noise outside our house. It sounded like something was wrong with our son and I told Tony to see what it was, but he wouldn't make a move and then it was down to me.

I still had the first 'pot' up to my knee and I wasn't supposed to put weight through the leg, but I got myself up from the kitchen table and I hobbled my way down the hall with Tony following me.

When we got to the front door there was Reg holding our son in the air by his throat, his poor little legs were dangling down and his face was turning purple. We shouted for Reg to leave him alone and when Reg let him go our son went and hid behind me.

Then Reg started 'gobbing' at us and the more he shouted the worse he got, so I picked up a brick that was next to the step and I hit him over the head with it. He punched me back and he hit me so hard I would have been knocked to the ground if my son weren't behind me. He caught me before I could fall and I was still on my feet when Reg went off to his own house.

As soon as Reg had gone Tony told our son to go to his room, and when our son was safely out of the way I dared Tony to tell me what kind of a man would just stand there and watch while another man strangled his son. And what kind of a man would just stand there and watch while another man punched his disabled wife?

Tony defended himself by trying to tell me Reg was too drunk to know what he'd been doing, and the only reason he hadn't hit him was because he could have killed him. I told him that was even more of a reason why he should have sorted Reg out and Tony defended himself by 'battering' me.

'Battering' me might have made him feel better about himself but it didn't stop our neighbours and friends from hearing what Reg had done to our son. Before long there were loads of people coming round to ask Tony why Reg was still walking, when they would have killed anyone that so much as tried to lay a finger on one of their kids.

When Tony tried to defend himself with the same excuses he'd given me, our neighbours would always walk away in total disgust and then Tony would always 'batter' me for what they'd thought of him. But whatever anyone did think of him, or whatever Reg was ready to do to us, nothing stopped Tony from having his Saturday nights with Reg's wife. On one of those Saturday nights I heard loads of banging, clattering and smashing going off outside our house.

When I looked out the window there was Reg smashing down our six-foot fence. That fence had been put in with concrete blocks and it went all the way round our house, but it still wasn't strong enough or long enough to stop Reg from breaking it down, and when every bit of our fence was flat Reg came round to our back door where he started hammering and yelling, "I'm going to kill you!" And "I'm going to kill your kids!"

My youngest son Philip had gone off to play with a mate so I wasn't worried for him, but I wasn't going to just sit there and wait for Reg to break in and kill me. I went to call the police and I only just got to the phone when it rang. It was my eldest son Mark phoning me up for a chat and when he heard all the noise over the phone he asked me what it was.

I told him what Reg had done to our fence and the noise he could hear over the phone was Reg trying to break in and kill me. Then I told him I'd just been going to phone the police when he rang and my son told me not to, because he said he was coming right away and he would sort it out.

I should have felt safe until my son got to me because all our doors were really strong and we'd put metal screens over our windows after we'd been burgled when we first moved into Buttershaw. But I couldn't just sit there and wait for my son and I told him I was going to phone the police anyway.

Then as soon as he got off the phone I rang 999, but the police didn't come when they said they would, so I rang them up again and they still didn't sound like they wanted to come, until I told them Reg's name and why they had to send him to jail. That got them to listen, and they promised me they were on their way but my eldest son got to my house before the police could arrive.

He was a lot smaller and lighter than Reg but he got him away from our back door, which should have told Reg to be careful with how he behaved with my son but instead of going back to his own home Reg went to grab my son by his ears and that was the biggest mistake he could ever have made.

My son had suffered with years of pain and infections in his ears. If anyone ever went anywhere near his ears it always sent him 'loopy' and before Reg could make another move on my son, he'd been grabbed and dragged all the way round the house and into our front garden.

From where I was in the house I could hear my son asking Reg why was he doing all of this to me when I was just as much of a victim as he was, and if he wanted to have a go at anyone, then he should be having a go at Tony. But by that time Reg was too far off his head to listen to sense and he tried to go back for another go at breaking in on me.

Next thing Reg was being dragged down the road and I was doing my best to follow. It was all muddy and slippery-wet from when it had been raining. What with a slippery road and a 'pot' on my leg I had no chance of keeping up, and by the time I did catch up my son had dragged Reg all the way around the corner to our local shop, where he'd beaten him up so bad you couldn't tell who it was when you looked at his face.

When loads of police finally came, they put Reg into someone's house while they questioned us and after we'd told them what they wanted to know they arrested Reg and took him away, leaving us free to go off to my son's flat. That's where we were when the police came back that night bringing their one idiot with them.

Thank God there aren't many like him in the police because he was the sort of 'Copper' that gives 'real' policemen a bad name. He was the kind of idiot who always makes things worse when he opens his mouth and he got right on my nerves when he said, "You know he could do you for assault! Have you seen the state of his face! You could get done for assault!"

That was the daftest thing I'd ever heard anyone say to a person who'd just saved someone from an assault and I told him not to be so stupid. Then I asked him how my son could be done for assault when Reg had started it all and my son was only protecting his mother when he'd finished off what Reg had started? Was he supposed to just stand there and watch while Reg broke in and killed me?

When I ended up with asking the idiot who did he think would be stupid enough to try and say it was my son who'd done the assault, a 'proper' policeman gave me a 'look' that said 'take no notice of him'. Then he took his stupid mate away and that was the last we heard about Reg until the following morning, when the police came back to say that Reg wasn't pressing charges. And just before they left, one of them said that none of them could understand how someone as small as my son could have made such a mess of Reg's face.

Next thing it was Tony's turn to come sneaking up to the flat wearing a stupid old coat of his dad's and his dad's old flat cap and glasses We all burst out laughing when Tony said, "I'm in disguise! No one will recognise me! Will they?"

That was the most stupid thing that any of us had ever heard, and when we'd all finished laughing at Tony I told him I was never going back to live in that house. All that I wanted was to go and get my bloody stuff and Tony just agreed with me.

My eldest son borrowed a van off a mate and Tony helped us to empty the house. We stored most of my small stuff in his mum's 'box' (small) bedroom and my big stuff got stored in my son's flat where I also stayed for a couple of days before moving in with Tony at his mum's house.

I had to share a room and a bed with Tony, which was all right with me because his mum was a right 'telly' (Television) addict that used to stay up nearly all night every night just watching 'telly'. Had he tried to rape or 'batter' me his mum would have heard him, and if there was one thing Tony would never want it was his mum finding out what he was really like.

As his mum had a phone in her house it should have been a lot easier for me to talk to the Solicitor about my divorce, but if Tony weren't hovering around his mum would be ear wigging for him. So I got in touch with Eileen who phoned the Solicitor for me and then all I had to do was get a place of my own.

Getting a place of my own turned out to be much harder than I thought it was going be. All the Council could offer me was a Bedsit, which was no good for someone in a wheelchair with a child to look after. And when they told me it could take them months and months to find me somewhere suitable I knew I had to go private. But I couldn't drive with a knee-length 'pot' so I had to get Tony to drive 'Us' to look for 'Our' new home.

'We' went to see loads of different places, some of which were too far for our son to get to school, others were much too expensive for what they were like and I was beginning to give up hope. Then a house came up on Overton Drive and the moment I saw it I fell in love with it.

As soon as we went inside I just knew exactly where every bit of my furniture was going to go and I had to have that house. The only problem was that 'We' didn't have the money for the first week's rent, or to put down for the Bond, so Tony went to his sister, Mary, who lent 'him' the money and then 'I' moved into Overton Drive-without Tony.

Moving into Overton Drive without Tony in December of 1993 was the most perfect Christmas present that I could have asked for. For the first time in too many years there was no one to tell me what I could or what I couldn't do. There was no big cloud called Tony hovering over us. My eldest son, his friends and all my friends were finally free to visit me for a chat, or a drink, or a meal, or all three. I was free to do and say what I wanted without being 'nattered', 'battered', mocked and raped.

And then in the early part of the New Year I was finally set free from my permanent period after it suddenly got heavier and heavier so that I had to be rushed into the BRI where a lady surgeon by the name of Jones gave me a hysterectomy.

The operation went well. There were no complications. I had a good recovery and as soon as I'd fully recovered I really started to live. From then on, every Friday, Saturday and Sunday night you'd find me out with my friends in Halifax. Tony still had my car because I couldn't drive it with a 'pot' on my leg, but most of the time there was someone to take me and if there wasn't, I'd just get myself a taxi.

The name of the first taxi driver to take me to Halifax is Kevin and we soon became such good friends he never charged me the fare to the Ring 'o' Bells. There I'd have a few drinks with my mates while we made up our minds on what nightclub we wanted and once we'd decided, my mates would give me a 'piggyback' up the road to the club.

Going to all those different nightclubs so regularly soon opened up my eyes and my ears to another side of life. Up until then I'd had no clue that men and women could feel so free with each other when they wanted to be with each other, and for the first time in my whole life I realised that I knew nothing at all about relationships. I'd never even heard of such things as giving a 'blowjob' or getting 'oral' and the more I thought the more I realised that all I knew about being intimate was rape and 'wham-bam-thank-you-mam'.

I'd lived for over forty years, been raped at eleven years of age, been forced into sex by my only fiancé, been raped and 'battered' by two husbands, had three children, one affair, and I'd nearly died from a brain haemorrhage, but I'd never had a 'normal' relationship, in the 'normal' way, with a 'normal' boyfriend.

Finally having the freedom to see and hear how ordinary people lived ordinary lives and having the space to think about what I'd had to do with my life got me to understand why I'd always thought of sex as boring. I'd never understood why women got so excited when they were expecting it, which then got me to wondering what sex would be like with a proper 'Starter', a 'Main Course', and a 'Dessert'.

Being over forty years of age meant I had a lot of catching up to do on how to have a proper relationship, and I knew the only way for anyone to learn about relationships was through having relationships. There was a time when I had a different boyfriend for every night of the week without there being anything sexual with any one of them.

Before I accepted any lad as a boyfriend I always let him know he wouldn't be the only one I was seeing. I always made it clear that if he wanted more than one night a week with me he couldn't have it. If he wanted more than a kiss and a cuddle he wouldn't get it. And if he couldn't keep to what I'd told him, I'd send him down the road.

That way I learned a lot about relationships in a very short time but my life wasn't all about nightclubs and boyfriends. I still had a young son who needed a dad and just because I'd 'kicked Tony into touch' didn't mean I was going to deprive our son of his dad, so I let Tony come round for his 'tea' every evening with his son.

But there are some people that you just can't be nice to without them taking the piss, and Tony was one of them. He was all right until he realised I was never going to let him get back in my life and then he soon went back to his stupid arguments that always ended up with me being 'battered' by him.

After just a little while of knowing he wasn't going to get back with me Tony's arguing got so bad that every evening I'd just dish up their 'tea' and tell him to leave when they'd finished and then I'd just go out and leave them to it.

Leaving Tony and our son to have their 'tea' without me being there did work out at first, but then Tony started waiting on me to come home and the longer I left it the longer he'd wait, which would always lead to another one of his arguments and to Tony 'battering' me.

I don't know how long Tony's arguing and 'battering' me in my own home would have gone on if it hadn't been for my eldest son, who must have realised what was happening, and then he started coming around a lot more often. Whenever my eldest son was at my house Tony would always back off, but he couldn't be there to protect me all of the time and I doubt if I would have coped if I hadn't made a 'total friend' I'd met in the Ring 'o' Bells when I first started my clubbing nights in Halifax.

From the moment we met we 'connected' and except for my mum he was and still is the only person I've ever known that always knows how I really feel, and in those days he phoned me every day in his lunch break just to see how I was. If he thought there was something wrong he'd just leave his work and come to my house, and one day when he rang me up Tony had hurt me so bad I was wondering when was it all going to end.

Though I did really try to hide how bad I felt, the next thing my 'total' friend was at my house. What started off as a cuddle for comfort led to a kiss, and then one thing led to another. That was in 1994 and nothing has ever spoiled our special and open relationship in which we've always been free to be with anyone else. But if one of us is with someone else, then it's always been 'hands off' and even if it is 'hands off' we've always been and still are free to meet up for a meal or a drink or a chat.

Some people might say we've only been using each other, and they are free to think or say what they want. All I have to say is that both of us had seen too many people who'd lived happy together until one of them wanted to get married. Once that piece of paper was signed and the ring was on the finger, one of them always seemed to want to own the other. Then they're clamped, and they can't do this and they can't do that.

We might be right or we might be wrong with the

way we've always been, but we must have got something right because our relationship has lasted nearly eighteen years and my life would have been close to perfect if it hadn't been for Tony who I had stopped from having his 'tea' with our son. And I'd only just threatened him with a Restraining Order but that didn't stop him from coming round one evening to ask me if I minded him getting changed to go out for some fun.

At the time our son, Philip was off playing football with his mates which meant I was all on my own in the house, and the last thing I wanted to do was start an argument by telling him no, so I said yes, expecting him to just leave when he'd finished. But once he'd showered and got changed Tony came and told me that I was always trying to stop him from going out and having fun when I was always going out whenever I wanted to have some fun.

That was such a stupid thing to say when I'd just let him have a shower and get changed. So I told him I couldn't give a shit about what he did or who he was doing it with, which made Tony so mad that he just walked up to me and punched me in the head as he shouted, "You'll never manage without me!"

He could have hit me anywhere on my body, but he just had to punch me on the same spot where he knew they'd clipped my aneurysm and he'd punched me so hard he damaged my neck and put my back out, sending me into the worst kind of agony.

Even though I was hurting so bad I still wasn't going to let Tony go back to his silly bitch, knowing how much he'd hurt me, so I fought back the pain enough to point my finger and shout, "You just watch me, Boy!"

Chapter Seventeen

It was about four o'clock in the afternoon when Tony punched me in the head, leaving me in so much pain that about an hour later I had to call out the Emergency Doctor, who did nothing much to help me. After I'd told him what Tony had done he just had a look at my head, gave me some painkillers, wrote a letter for my doctor, told me to call my own doctor- if I was still in pain in the morning, and then he just left me in the same pain he'd found me in.

I was used to handling a lot of pain, but this time it was so bad that when my youngest son came home from playing football with his mates about nine o'clock that night, he could see there was something really wrong with me and he asked me if I was all right. I couldn't tell him what his dad had done, so I told him I'd tripped in the kitchen and banged my head on the corner of the worktop.

My youngest son accepted my lie, and Tony would

have got away with it if the pain had gone away. But instead of getting better the pain kept getting worse, and I had a horrible night full of agony in my neck and my back. By morning my head felt like it was going to explode and I had no choice but to call my doctor's surgery, where they arranged for Dr Corbridge to call in and see me while she was doing her 'rounds'.

It was about midday when Dr Corbridge got to me and Tony came so soon after she arrived that he almost followed her into the house. That meant I couldn't tell my doctor what he'd done to me, so I just handed her the Emergency Doctor's letter and after she'd finished reading the letter Dr Corbridge asked me how I'd got hurt.

As Tony was listening to every word I had no choice but to tell her the same lie I'd told my youngest son, and when I'd finished telling her how I'd tripped in the kitchen and banged my head on the corner of the worktop Dr Corbridge just gave me a little wink that let me know she knew the truth.

But you wouldn't have known she knew about Tony from the way she talked to him, or from the way she examined me, or from the way she wrote me a letter to take to Casualty, or from the way she asked Tony if he was going to take me to the BRI or did she have to call an ambulance.

Everything she'd done had been in such a clever way that Tony never had a clue she could see right through his loving, caring husband act when he was telling her there was no need for an ambulance, and of course he'd take me to Casualty, where I gave them the letter Dr Corbridge had written for them.

When it came to my turn to be examined they took us into a small room with curtains opposite the door. The curtains were opened up on a space where doctors and nurses kept coming and going. One of those doctors coming and going was 'J' (Dr Wright) from Ward 5, and when Tony saw 'J' he got into a right state. He knew that if 'J' saw me he'd come straight over to talk to me, and that was something Tony couldn't risk. So every time 'J' made a move to where he might see me, Tony would move between us.

He was so good at blocking me off that 'J' never caught a glimpse of me before they took me away to the X-Ray room. Tony tried to come in with me but the nurses told him he couldn't, and as soon as they'd shut the door on him they couldn't wait to tell me that everyone knew what he'd done.

They said that Dr Corbridge's letter had told them everything they needed to know about what had happened to me, and they asked me if I wanted to call the police. But silly me was so worried what our son would think of his dad that I told them no, and the only help I took from them was an appointment to see a Consultant.

The appointment was made for following day and though Tony took me to it he couldn't stay to go in with me. He had his own important appointment, which I think had something to do with the sale of the Café and that meant I got to see the Consultant without Tony hovering over us.

Being able to see the Consultant on my own gave

me the chance to talk freely, and after I told him my biggest fear was that Tony's punch might have damaged my brain he told me not to worry. He said there was nothing wrong with my brain or the clip on the aneurysm, and he even showed me the X-Rays to prove it.

But the news on my neck and my back was not as good as the news on my brain. The Consultant told me that the force of the punch had given me 'Whiplash' in the neck, and the way I'd been hit had put out a disc in my lower back. He said I'd suffered the same kind of damage I could have got from a bad car crash, and he'd referred me for Physio to see if that would help.

Just before the end of my appointment he asked me if I was sure that I didn't want the police involved, and when silly me said that I didn't he told me they'd written everything down in my Medical Records, which they would let me have if ever I changed my mind and wanted Tony 'done'.

So there was nothing to let Tony know that anyone knew what he'd done to me when he picked me up from the BRI. But all the attention I'd had from the different doctors and nurses must have frightened him because when we got back to Overton Drive he just dropped me off and he never came back to my house, though he did ring me up a lot.

Most of the talking we did on the phone had to do with our son, but I also told him I wanted my car, which he refused to give me back. He knew that with the car being registered in his name I couldn't ask the police to go and get it for me, but that didn't mean I was going to let him keep it. All the payments on the car were coming out of my Mobility Allowance, and if I stopped the payments they'd want all the money in one lump sum or they'd take my car away from him, and I knew Tony wouldn't be able to get the money. So I stopped all of the payments.

Once that problem was out of the way, I would have been able to get some fun back into my life if it wasn't for the pain in my neck and my back. Physio was helping to keep me moving, but it wasn't getting rid of the constant pain and I kept thinking I would have to live with it for the rest of my life. Then I remembered how Acupuncture had helped me with the horrible shoulder pain that a lot of people get after a stroke.

There was no Acupuncture on the NHS (National Health Service) in those days and I'd had to go private, but it was worth it. The Acupuncturist I'd found got rid of my shoulder pain, and I still had her number so I rang her up, and when I told her about the disc in my back she told me what I really needed was an Osteopath. She gave me the number for one that she could recommend.

The Osteopath put the disc back and after about four or five months of slowly easing pain, I was back to my old self again. By that time Tony's mum had been forced to sell her home to pay off the rest of the debts on the Café, and she had to rent a bungalow that needed a lot of decorating before it was fit to live in. I had nothing against Tony's mum, so I'd gone to help her out and it was while we were doing the decorating that Tony's mum told me how she'd been letting Tony

189

and Reg's wife spend their nights at her house.

That meant the room and the bed I'd shared with Tony was the same room and the same bed he'd been using to sleep with Reg's wife, and there isn't a way I can say how I felt about that, or how I felt about the fact that my own mother-in-law had helped her son to cheat on the mother of her grandchildren.

All I can say is that I couldn't stand to be anywhere near Tony's mum any longer than I had to, and as I was rushing to leave I told her I never wanted to see or speak to her ever again, which I wouldn't have done if she hadn't phoned me one day to tell me that Tony was threatening to kill himself.

I didn't know if Tony was serious or if he was just looking for sympathy. But I did know that if he killed himself, his son would have to live with it and it would ruin the rest of his life. So I agreed to talk to him and when I got to the bungalow I gave the Tony the biggest 'bollocking' of his life.

Instead of trying to be all 'nice' with him I told him what a selfish bastard he'd always been, and that if he went ahead and killed himself it would be the most selfish thing he could do to his son who would have to spend the rest of his life knowing his dad had killed himself. But if he was selfish enough to kill himself, then he should go ahead and do it because I didn't care if he lived or died.

Then it was his mum's turn and I said to her that she was to blame for Tony being the way that he was. If it wasn't for her always sticking up for his 'arse' when she knew he was in the wrong, he wouldn't be the way that he was, and that she as his mother should be the one to sort him out.

I finished off by telling them both that I never wanted to see them ever again, and when I said I was washing my hands of the pair of them for the very last time, there was a look of total shock on their faces. But the shock I'd given them was nothing to the shock they were going to get when Reg found out his wife was still sleeping with Tony at his mum's house.

The way I heard it was that when Tony saw Reg coming up to the house he climbed out of a downstairs window at the back, and he never stopped running his way round the back of all the houses until he'd reached his sister's home.

While Tony was doing all of his running and hiding, Reg smashed up every single door and window in the house and when he'd finished with smashing up the house he made such a mess of the car it was a total 'write-off'. That was the end of my car and my life with Tony.

He wasn't going to sign the papers for our divorce until I went down to the bungalow and threatened to show the Court my Medical Records, as well as getting Dr Corbridge and the Consultant to testify against him in Court in front of all our old neighbours, our families and the kids. That soon got him to sign the papers and then my divorce didn't take long to come through.

Once Tony was out of my life for good I was free to have loads of fun and loads of laughs which was really easy for me. I'd made a lot of friends while I'd been living at Overton Drive and one of my best friends, aside from my 'total' friend, was the first taxi driver to take me back to the Ring 'o' Bells, when I'd first started my clubbing nights in Halifax.

His name is Kevin and we'd soon become such good friends that he never charged me or the lads for taking us anywhere we needed to go, even though in those days there was always a proper boyfriend on the scene. The only trouble with most of them was that they couldn't keep to what we'd agreed and they'd try to move in with me, which is exactly what happened with a boyfriend called Andy, who thought he was going to marry me.

I'd been going out with Andy for quite a few months before my eldest son asked me if I wanted to buy some holiday tickets and take his brother to Spain. One of his workmates had a daughter who'd been going to Spain with a friend, but her friend had been taken ill and his daughter didn't want to go on her own, so I bought their holiday off them.

That was in the early part of October. I had my birthday in Benidorm and what a brilliant birthday it was with just the two of us. But when we got home I got a right shock when I found my wedding dress and veil was hanging outside my wardrobe. I hadn't put them there and I couldn't understand it until I went into the Hare and Hounds pub where it was all congratulations.

When I asked them what it was all about they told me I was getting married to Andy. They said he'd even asked our local Vicar who used the pub, if he would marry us. And he'd asked a lad we both knew from the pub if he would be Best Man. It seemed like the only one who didn't know about my wedding was me, so that was the end for Andy, and I can't remember if I was going out with my next boyfriend, John when my friend Kevin first found out he was going blind.

Going blind meant Kevin had to spend a lot more of his time in the office and he had a lot of problems without having anyone he could to talk to. He'd been a good friend to me and the taxi office was only five minutes walk from the house. So I used to go down to the office and sit with them at night if I wasn't going out through the week, which I could have been with John.

John had his own place and the only times he stayed over at my house was when we'd been out somewhere together. Our relationship was working well and we'd been together for quite a few months when my left leg suddenly started getting colder and colder. The colder it got the more painful it was, and if I tried to warm it up the pain would get so bad it was next to unbearable, even if I was only using a leg warmer.

Over the next couple of months the leg got so bad I could hardly walk on it at all, and I had to spend most of my time laid down with my leg raised. That meant there were a lot of household and personal things I couldn't do for myself, so John began to stay a lot more often with me and Kevin was always popping in to see if I needed any help from him.

With all of the rest my leg was getting, I thought it would have got better but instead the leg got to where it was so painful I couldn't stand it any more and I had to ask for a home visit from Dr Corbridge. The night before she came, the pain was so bad that John stayed up the whole night with me.

John was still sitting up with me when Dr Corbridge came to the house and when she checked the pulses in the leg she got straight on the phone to the BRI where they found me a bed and they'd booked me into the Vascular Ward before Dr Corbridge got off the phone.

John took me straight to the Vascular Ward where the Consultant Mr Wilkinson came to examine my leg. He ordered loads of different tests and after all the tests were in, he came back on the Ward to tell me that the main veins in my groin and stomach were all blocked, and that out of the three main veins in my leg two of them were blocked.

He said he was going to try and clear all the blockages in the hope that the third vein in my leg would be healthy enough to take the blood to my feet. He did warn me it might not work but he had to give it a try or I would have to lose my leg. That really worried me because there were loads of amputees on the Ward. But I needn't have worried because I'd got lucky again. Mr Wilkinson was such a brilliant Vascular Surgeon that he cleared out all the blockages from all the veins and he saved my leg. My leg warmed up, I could walk without pain and then I went home to deal with John whom I'd trusted with my money.

When I'd gone into the Vascular Ward I'd given John all my money for the weekly bills and the shopping. But when my eldest son, Mark had gone to him for some shopping money there was nothing left. John had spent it all on himself except for some of my money he'd used to buy me a pair of earrings. He'd bought the earrings in the Hare and Hounds, where he'd also told all of my friends that both my sons were his. That was such a weird thing to do I had to get rid of John before he went and did something that was even worse than stealing my money and pretending my kids were his.

Finding out there was something really wrong with John in time was a lucky break for me, but the next break in my life wasn't lucky because I went and broke my left leg during a night out with my eldest son's girlfriend, Michelle. We were on our way out of the Halfway House pub in Queensbury when Michelle stumbled on the couple of stone steps that led down from the entrance and onto the street. I thought Michelle was going to fall and as I tried to save her from falling my left leg went from under me.

I was the one who ended up with falling down the steps and when I got up I couldn't put any weight on my left leg, so Michelle and the Landlord of the Halfway House helped me to hop my way down to the next street where Michelle's mother lived, and I went straight to bed without thinking there was anything wrong with the leg.

There was no pain overnight and I had a really sound sleep. But when I woke up next morning and tried to straighten the leg, the scream I gave from the pain was so loud it woke up everyone in the house. My son ran in to see what was wrong with me and after I told him how bad my leg hurt he went and got the others to help me get dressed.

As soon as they had me dressed, my son carried me down the stairs and he took me to the BRI, where they found I'd broken my leg in two places. They wanted to put a full 'pot' on my leg, which meant I'd have to stay in the BRI until it had healed. So thank God Mr Bollen was there because he let me have a half 'pot' and a leg stretcher (extended leg rest) for my wheelchair, and it was thanks to him that I could go straight back to having some fun in my life.

Chapter Eighteen

Overton Drive turned into one big party house after my eldest son, Mark split up with his girlfriend and moved in with me and his brother, Philip. I'd made lots of friends and both my sons had loads of mates who all treated me like a mum. I was always cooking for loads of people and we were always having a laugh.

Lots of my sons' friends had no one at home they could turn to, so they would bring me all their problems and I would help with working them out- especially when it was something that they couldn't tell their parents, which happened all the time. Though they were all good kids at heart none of them were angels and they did all sorts of silly things that young people do when they're learning all about life.

Some of the things they did were so silly that you couldn't help but laugh, like the Christmas time when they'd been having a drink and then gone off to the shop in our local petrol station. But instead of just getting what they went for, the lads 'lifted' loads of stuff that none of us needed, and a bag of coal was one such thing because my house had central heating.

I don't know if the bag of coal was ripped when the lads 'lifted' it or if it got torn when they were carrying it back to the house, but however it happened the lads left a long trail of coal behind them and I had to laugh at their state and the trail of coal to the house. But even though I had a laugh I did put them right about what they'd done because every time they did something wrong I would always tell them why and they always respected me for being straight with them.

Between my friends and my sons' mates there were brilliant times at Overton Drive and my boyfriend was brilliant as well. His name was Michael and he was wonderful with me. Every Saturday and Sunday morning he'd bring me a cup of tea. When I was ready to eat he'd make all the breakfasts and then he'd bring me mine in bed. Michael would always help me with everything and when it came to Christmas time he'd be up and have all the housework done before anyone else woke up.

The first Christmas we spent together was the first time Michael had ever been to a Pantomime and he loved it. Both of my sons were all right with Michael and we took him to loads of nice places he'd never been to before he met me. And he took me to visit my mum when I wanted to put a wreath on her grave.

He was the best boyfriend I've ever had and I really do believe that we would still be together if it wasn't for my eldest son falling out with him when his girlfriend's grandma died. They'd just buried her grandma and they'd been having the 'Wake' in a pub, but instead of respecting her grandma the family started fighting, which really upset my son.

He thought her family had shown him up, and when the two of them came back to Overton Drive my son started an argument. His arguing got so bad that at one point he pushed himself so close to her it looked like he was going to hit her, which he wasn't going to do.

The reason he'd pushed himself so close was because he wanted to shout in her face, which wasn't right when she'd only just buried her grandma. When we told him to leave her alone and let her grieve in peace, he wouldn't. So Michael pushed him into the hallway and all the way up the stairs. From that moment on my son hated Michael so much that he gave me an ultimatum that it was either him or Michael, and what could I do but choose my son, because your children are for life.

I could have told Michael just to go but I didn't want to hurt him, and I had to find a way of making him want to leave me so I used his housemate Billy who was always in Michael's face telling him what to do. The way Billy rolled over him had everyone saying that Michael was 'Gay', and I was bisexual for being with him.

Now don't get me wrong, because as far as I'm concerned anyone can be as 'Gay' or bisexual as they want to be and it doesn't bother me, but being called something I'm not is really upsetting to me. Though I had told Michael how I felt, he did nothing to change the way he behaved with Billy and I made it all sound a lot worse than it was by pretending to talk in my sleep.

I talked in my sleep all the time and Michael knew that I did, so I pretended I was talking in my sleep one night when I said how making people call me bisexual was hurting me worse than it was. And how it had hurt me so much that I'd stopped wanting to be with him. And this hurt Michael so much that he went ahead and left me.

Making Michael leave me was one of the hardest things I've ever had to do in my life. What made it worse was the following week my son's girlfriend moved out of Overton Drive, and the week after that my son followed her, which meant I never did have to break up with Michael. I tried my best to get back with him but every time I tried to approach him Michael would always run away, and to this day I still believe that forcing Michael to leave me was the biggest mistake of my life.

I was still struggling to cope with his loss when dad's girlfriend died. Both dad and Marion had been poorly for a long time and they'd both been in and out of hospital. Dad was in hospital from having had a heart attack and a stroke when Marion died.

With dad being so blind he couldn't live in the flat on his own and when he was well enough to be discharged he went straight from hospital to a Nursing Home. I wasn't involved in choosing the home so I don't know if it was planned or just a lucky chance that my daughter managed the Home.

The name of Home was Beckfield and it had its own Social Club with a bar that held dances for the residents as well darts and dominoes. They could all go out whenever they wanted, but there's nothing like being with your own family so I asked my sons if they'd help me with their granddad if he stayed with us at weekends.

When my sons agreed to help me we set up the dining room for dad. Then every Friday to Sunday evening he would stay with us, and was always in floods of tears when Sunday evening came. I felt so sorry for him every Sunday evening, but I couldn't look after him on my own.

The best I could do for my dad was make his weekends special and that's why we took him to places he loved and remembered, like the seaside at Bridlington. We also took him to loads of different places he'd never been to before as well as anywhere else he wanted to go, which really surprised my writing helper who wanted to know why was I so good with my dad when he'd been so bad with me.

The reason I gave to my writing helper was that I still loved my dad. When I was little he'd spoiled me rotten, though he did make me work for my money. But that was only to teach me respect for the value of money because all the time I was growing up I never wanted for anything. There wasn't a time that I couldn't sit on dad's knee and get loads of cuddles from him. He'd taken me everywhere on the wagons with him. We were always playing in the warehouse together and he'd take us all over the East Coast on weekend trips and holidays.

If it weren't for dad and his great uncle's farm I would never have learned to ride and look after horses which I still love to this very day, and I still remembered how every Thursday he'd bought me loads of sweets. I loved my dad for how he'd been with me when I was growing up and that could never stop. Disowning me when I got pregnant and then forcing me to get married was just the way they were in those days.

That's why I couldn't hate my dad for being what he'd only been brought up to be, though I did ask him why he'd cheated on mum when she'd loved him so much. Dad told me that he never loved another woman the way he'd loved my mum, but she was the only woman he'd ever been with and he always thought he was missing out by never having been with another woman.

He said he knew he'd been a fool and that he wished he'd never done it, but being sorry didn't stop dad from chasing women, because he hadn't been in Beckfield very long before he got himself a girlfriend who also lived in the Home. I don't know how old she was at the time, but my dad was over seventy years of age which didn't seem to matter because they weren't too old to be 'at it'. In fact they were 'at it' so much I had to go to Beckfield for a meeting after they asked for a double bed in a double room. They were always falling out of the single bed they were sharing.

Whether they got what they wanted or whether they didn't is something I don't remember any more because there was a lot more for me to worry about when dad found out that someone was cleaning out his Bank Account. He believed it was my brother but I have no proof of that. All I can say is what my dad told me, and this is the way it went.

He said my brother had taken over managing his account because he was too blind to read his statements from the Bank, or what was on his cheques. Any time there were bills to be paid my brother would make out the cheques and then he'd put the pen in dad's hand and guide it for him to sign.

Up until then the only money he'd spent from the sale of the bungalow was the money he'd used to do up Marion's house, which they'd sold when the house got too much for them and they'd rented a flat instead. That meant there should have been most of the money from the sale of two houses in his bank account, plus what wasn't stolen from mum's cabinet on the night she went and died. Before he'd gone into Beckfield dad never went to the bank, but once he was in the Home he got someone to take him there every week. That's how and when he found out that loads of money was missing from his account and he blamed my brother for it.

I can't say that I blame dad for blaming my brother. But at the same time I can't say that my brother was taking the money. What I can say is that dad had owned the bungalow outright and Marion's home was paid for. Dad had always kept all of his bills, and later on when his Will had been read I asked dad's Solicitor to get all of his statements from the Bank. When we'd checked them against all of his bills there was nothing that matched by hundreds and hundreds of pounds.

That was after dad had died, but while he was still alive there were loads of things that made him believe my brother had taken the money, and he got himself into such a state that by the time he asked me to take him to see his Solicitors I wouldn't let him go.

I said if it really was my brother I hoped the money would burn him and ruined his frigging life. I told him I wasn't going to take him to see his Solicitor, or anywhere else to do with the missing money because I wasn't going to lose him over a bit of money, so he could just calm down.

Once I had taken over with paying his bills, dad did calm down enough to have a good time with us, until one night about ten o'clock when the Home phoned to tell me he was in the hospital dying from a heart attack and a stroke. Then the hospital rang to tell me he didn't have long to live and if I wanted to see him before he died I would have to get there soon. This all came as such a shock that the first person I called was Michael. I know we weren't together any more, but when I phoned him and told him what was going on he gave me a lift to the hospital and he stopped with me as well.

By the time my brother and his wife arrived, dad had been in and out of consciousness. But as soon as my brother said, "Hello dad. How are you?" he came round like a shot and threw two punches straight at my brother's chin. Though dad was blind and dying at the time, both of his punches came so close to hitting his son right on the chin you could see my brother's beard quiver.

Missing my brother made dad so mad he started shouting and yelling at his son to get out. His carrying on got so bad I had to tell the staff to keep my brother away from us. From then until my dad was dead my brother and his wife kept to themselves. They slept in a bed in the relative's room while I stopped up all night with my dad and I even felt guilty when I had to leave him to go to the toilet.

When the shift changed about eight o'clock in the morning I was still with my dad and I would have stopped with him if the staff hadn't kept telling me to go home for a rest and something to eat. They kept saying the way dad was he could last for ages and in the end I gave into them, which I still wish I hadn't, because I'd only been gone for an hour and a half at the most when the hospital rang to tell me dad had passed away.

The time between my leaving his bedside and dad dying was so short that it got me to wondering if dad couldn't die as long as I was with him. Then I got on to wondering what could have got him so angry with my brother that was prepared to use up his last bit of strength to kill him.

That was something I couldn't work out until I went to the home to collect his personal things. Then it got clearer when the staff told me what happened to dad on the day before he died. They said he had drawn out £500.00 when they'd taken him down to the bank that day. No one knew what the money was for, but dad never had less than £400.00 in his wallet and that had always been his way from when he'd first started working at Bradford Waste with his uncles.

They also said that my brother had been to see dad soon after they brought him back from the Bank. From what my brother had told the staff about the time he left the home, and from what the staff told us about the time they'd found dad on the floor of his room, there were only minutes between my brother leaving the Home and the staff finding my dad dying from a heart attack and a stroke.

Although he'd only just drawn out the £500.00 from the bank there was only a 'fiver' (£5.00) in dad's wallet when the staff gave it to me. But I still can't say my brother took all his money and left him to die because I wasn't there when it happened. And I wasn't there when someone was taking so much money from dad's account there was only £8,000.00 left from the sale of two houses, and what wasn't stolen when my mum had died. Anyway, there are only two things I have left to say about my brother and money.

The first is that I've never known anyone show themself up so much over money as when the Funeral Director came to see me and my brother at Overton Drive. For the most part, my brother just sat there saying nothing. But every time something came up that was going to cost some money, like the casket, flowers, and the music, he'd butt in with, "Oh! We don't want to be spending too much on that!"

I don't think the Funeral Director had ever met anyone like him, and he couldn't hide his disgust for my brother when he tried to get his hands on the

£60.00 Government Grant for the funeral by saying he should get the £60.00 Government Grant because he was unemployed. If both of our looks could have killed he would have been dead on the spot.

The second was that when it came to dad's Wake, my brother didn't put a penny towards it. I was the one who paid for it all and I made all the food myself. My brother paid his respects by bringing his wife to the Wake, where the pair of them ate like scavengers that hadn't eaten for weeks. Now that's enough about my brother, and all that's left to say about dad's funeral is that we buried him in the same grave as mum, and if there is a life beyond the grave I hope they're both as happy now as they were in their early life together.

Burying my dad next to my mum so soon after losing Michael marked the end of four brilliant years at Overton Drive, and my last few months weren't a patch on the rest. When I'd first moved into the house on Overton Drive the landlord had told me I could stay in the house. He told me he'd make me a sitting tenant, but he never stuck to his word and he kept on raising the rent even though there were lots of things wrong with the house that he just wouldn't repair.

The gas boiler for the central heating wasn't right and I was always afraid of suffocating from carbon monoxide poisoning. The windows were all rotting away and they were all in need of replacing. The front door was stuck shut and you couldn't get out if there was a fire or any emergency. When I tried to get him to put things right the landlord kept putting the house up for sale and then he'd take it off again. In the end I got so fed up of all the people coming round to view my home that I called in Environmental Health and they condemned the place.

Once the house was condemned, the landlord couldn't rent it out to anyone else and the Agents in charge of letting the house told me the only way he could sell it was by putting it in an auction. They also told me to stop paying them the extra money for the rent because they didn't trust him to give me back my bond.

I couldn't keep living with all that uncertainty so I went to the Council who gave me a flat in Queensbury. The flat was in such a horrible state I hated it from the moment I saw it. Both of my sons and my latest boyfriend Arthur also thought it was a right dump, but what could I do when I needed a home?

Chapter 19

Though there wasn't a thing in the flat the Council gave me on Hillcrest Avenue, in Queensbury, it stank something rotten. The previous tenants were drug addicts and had loads of dogs they'd let piss wherever they wanted. The whole place was infested with mice, which meant we had to find all the holes and block them off with foil because mice don't like the feel of foil on their teeth.

When they fitted the flat with central heating they'd left the old airing cupboard and hot water cylinder in the living room so my youngest son Philip knocked the whole lot down. Then my eldest son Mark levelled the floor where the cupboard had been, and both of them plastered the walls.

Ripping out all the old skirting boards and replacing them with new ones got rid of the stink that was left by the dogs, but the kitchen units, cupboards and worktops weren't safe to be used for food so we changed them all for new ones. And when it came to the decorating my eldest son's girlfriend 'mucked' in with us.

A lot of hard work went into that flat and when it was done it was beautiful, only I never got the chance to relax and enjoy what we'd done before I started having fits. I'd gone to spend some time with my eldest son Mark at his house, when I suddenly started shaking. It was the first fit I'd ever had and I thought my tablets might help, but I'd left them all at the flat. Mark couldn't give me a lift because he'd been having a drink, so he rang up his brother and told him to meet me and then he got me a taxi back to the flat.

I was shaking so bad when I got to the flat my youngest son Philip had to help me out of the taxi. Even then I couldn't walk for the shaking and he had to help me into the flat- which someone must have seen because it wasn't long before the 'word' went round that I'd got so drunk my son had to carry me into my home.

They were just typical, narrow-minded people who always think the worst of everyone else, and I wonder what they would have said if they'd seen me with the breathlessness and projectile vomiting that came as the fits went on and on. Eventually, one of the fits was so bad that my son's girlfriend had to put me to bed while they waited for the ambulance that never took me to Casualty, because the fit had stopped by the time they got to me.

If Doctor Corbridge had still been my doctor she would have sent me to see Mr Towns, who'd told me to go back to see him if there were any more problems to do with my brain. But when I'd moved to Queensbury I had to sign on to a new medical practice and after I told my new doctor about the fits, all she did was leave me to sit there without a word from her.

There was no interest from her in what I'd said about the fits. There was no advice from her. There was no offer of any treatment and after a while of just sitting in front of her, looking and feeling stupid I said, "Well, I'll phone Mr Towns, if you don't want to help me!" And she just replied with, "Mr Towns'll be too busy to see you!"

She couldn't have looked at my notes and she couldn't have known what Mr Towns was like, but she was going to find out. When his Secretary Ann had sent me my appointment, I took the letter to my new doctor's surgery and when someone come out of her office I marched in and slammed the letter down on her desk with, "I thought you said Mr Towns would be too busy to see me."

After my new doctor looked at the letter, her mouth went open and shut and when she'd got over the shock she shouted at me, "What are you doing in my office?"

If throwing me out of her office was her idea of medical treatment for fits, I thank God for Mr Towns. In no time at all he knew what was causing my fits and within four or five months of taking the tablets he put me on, my fits went away for good. The problems I had with my stomach and bowel had nothing to do with the fits, and I had to go back to my new doctor who diagnosed me with an ulcer and put me on some tablets.

The tablets she gave were just good enough help for me to go on an Austrian holiday with Arthur whom I'd met in the Ring o Bells. I was still living at Overton Drive when we met and we were together about a year and a half when we'd booked our holiday. Arthur was a lovely man who used to take me to the theatre and concerts and we were always going away to the coast for holidays.

I really did like Arthur, but he had one really bad habit that always drove me mad. Every time we had somewhere to go he always left the most important things until the very last moment. I don't know if he did it just to wind me up, or if it was just the way he was made. Whatever the reason it got on my nerves until I couldn't take any more and before we'd booked our holiday I'd told him that when we got back he would have to go.

Even then he went and wound me up on the day we were due to catch the coach. All I needed was packed and ready to go, including an overnight bag for a one night stop in Germany. All that was left for me to do was to get up, get showered, and get dressed. But Arthur left loads of things until the very last moment, including getting our money exchanged.

With all the last minute running around that Arthur had to do, he never had the time for a shower before we had to catch the coach and by the time we got to Germany his socks stank the whole room out. When I told him to get his socks out of the room Arthur just put them into the bin and I made him throw them out the window.

It was the very last straw for me and the night we got back from Austria I made Arthur sleep on the couch. When I woke up during the night, Arthur was back in bed with me. It made me so mad I got out of bed and went to sleep in my son's, but even that didn't work with Arthur. Next thing he was back in bed with me and I nearly strangled him. And then the following morning he annoyed me again when at first he wouldn't take his clothes with him, but by the time I'd finished with Arthur all his clothes were gone along with him.

Nearly two years after I'd made Arthur take his clothes and leave, the problems I'd had with my stomach and bowel were worse than when my new doctor had diagnosed me with an ulcer. I was still taking the tablets she'd put me on and even though I wasn't a doctor I knew it was more than an ulcer. I was always on the toilet and my stool was always black. When I went back and asked to see a Consultant, all she said to me was, "You don't need a Consultant. What you need is to go away and keep taking the tablets."

When I went away like that doctor said, I was so desperate I told my friends what was going on with my stomach and bowel, and they had a word with one of their friends. His name was Dr Reynolds and he was such a lovely, caring man that he phoned me up himself. And what I told him over the phone concerned him so much that he gave me an urgent appointment.

I'd got really lucky in getting such a brilliant Consultant as Dr Reynolds. All it took was that one appointment for him to find a lump in my bowel, which he thought might be a cyst. Next thing I was in the BRI where they did test after test on me. The tests went on for about two weeks, and the last test was a Barium Enema at St Lukes Hospital.

When all the test results were in I got really lucky again. The General Surgeon (Colorectal Surgery Specialist) whom Dr Reynolds sent me to see was one of the very best. His name is Mr Griffith and he was the one who had to tell me the lump on my bowel was in a place with a million to one shot of getting one there. They couldn't really tell what it was without an operation, but the place it was in was so awkward to get at I might not survive the operation.

Being told that the operation could kill me was a really big shock, and even though I'd survived all of my other operations I was just as worried as anyone else would have been. But by that time, I knew enough to tell what a surgeon was like by the way they talked to you and the way they answered your questions. That was the way I knew that my life was in the best of hands with Mr Griffith, and I wanted the operation.

Once again I needn't have worried about an operation, because Mr Griffith got the lump out of one the most difficult places to get at, and he kept me alive to go back on the Ward with a partial ileostomy, a colostomy bag, and a bag over the end of my bowel. The only thing he couldn't do for me was to tell if the tumour was cancerous without sending it off for tests.

While I was under the anaesthetic I must have had another stroke. When I came round one side of my mouth had drooped. When I went to walk, my left leg kicked out and my left arm had gone all 'spastified' across my chest. When I tried to tell the doctor in charge of looking after me on the Ward that I must have had another stroke, she wouldn't listen to a word I had to say.

That doctor even refused to listen to all the other patients when they tried to tell her it was obvious I'd had another stroke by the way my arm, my leg and my mouth had changed from when I'd first come onto the Ward. So I don't know what kind of a doctor believes they know more about the way a patient's body behaves and feels than a patient they'd never even met before. All I can think is that she must have only glanced at my notes and thought I was just another typical stroke survivor.

I suppose I could have tried to get another opinion, but I was so worried the tumour was cancerous I couldn't think about anything else. The two weeks I had to wait for the test results to come back were some of the worst weeks I've ever spent in my life, and I can't explain how I felt when they told me the test results had shown them my tumour wasn't cancerous.

Once the threat of cancer was gone, I would have been having a chat and laugh with all the other patients and staff if it wasn't for the horrible nurse they'd put to watch over me. We'd never met before in our lives, but she went out of her way to make my life a misery and her attitude told me she must have hated me on sight.

Learning how to clean and take care of a colostomy bag with a spastified arm and only one good hand was a difficult, horrible job and she was such a difficult, horrible nurse that she wouldn't help me to learn how to do it on my own. Every time I asked for her help she'd shout at me with things like, "You're going to have to do it yourself!" and "I can't be doing it for you!"

The stress and depression I was getting from that awful nurse got even worse when I found out that she was the one they'd put in charge of unstitching the bag from over the end of my bowel, and there wasn't a thing I could do about it. She and the Ward Sister were such really 'big mates' the Sister wouldn't have listened to me if I'd tried to tell her what she was like with me.

I got so stressed from thinking about her unstitching the bag and so afraid she'd take the chance to hurt me that I burst out crying when Kate and Sam from the ileostomy team came onto the Ward to talk to me. Both of them were so nice to me they managed to calm me down enough to tell them all about the nurse and why I believed she was going to hurt me on purpose.

Kate and Sam must have spoken to someone about the way that nurse was with me and how scared I was of her because her attitude did get better. Though they did let her take out the stitches, she didn't hurt me too much and then they transferred her to another Ward which totally changed my life.

Once she was gone I spent most of the rest of my time on the Ward having loads of chats and lots of laughs. This was just as well because it was only about a month after I got discharged that I was back on the Ward getting my partial ileostomy reversed, which was really lucky for me because some people have to wait years and years before they can get it done.

Some time between seeing Dr Reynolds and getting discharged I was sent to see Mr Wilkinson, the Vascular Surgeon who'd saved my leg. He told me they'd found an aneurysm in my stomach and they were going to have to keep a check on it, but I didn't have to worry because it was still too small to threaten my life.

My dad had an aneurysm in his stomach, and only about six months ago Mr Wilkinson told me that should have been passed down the male side of dad's family, and that the chances of it crossing to the female line were millions to one against. So it was just my luck to get the aneurysm instead of it going to my brother. Mr Wilkinson still keeps a check on it and I'm very happy to able to say it still hasn't grown too big.

Anyway, Mr Griffith was such a good surgeon he got me back to having a normal life without a Colostomy bag in no time at all, and I was just pegging out my washing one day when a woman called Barbara stopped for a chat. Barbara lived at the end of our Avenue and she was out walking her dog one day when she'd stopped to tell me that she didn't know how I managed to peg out washing with only one hand.

Barbara said that when she'd first seen me doing it she'd tried it out for herself and found she just couldn't do it with only one hand. She seemed so nice I told her to come on in and I'd teach her, but at first she wouldn't come in because she found the look of my dog Buster too scary for her.

Buster was only a pup at the time but he was an Irish Staffordshire Bull Terrier and bull terriers frighten lots of people. They've been given a bad reputation that most of them don't deserve because dogs are only as good or bad as their owners have trained them to be, and I'd learned to train dogs from when I was still only small, so Buster knew how to play without hurting anyone.

Another thing that made Buster so safe to be with was that when he'd been given to my son as a birthday present, he'd been taken from his mum too early and what with me having to feed him and treat him like a baby he'd grown to be such giddy fun that Barbara soon got so used to him that every time she came around, the two of them would end up playing together.

Barbara was only small and every time they played Buster would end up pinning her down which always gave us loads of laughs. Between the three of us we had so much fun that Barbara started coming round to help me with cleaning and sorting things out. After a while we started going down to the valley on long walks together and then I started going to Church with Barbara. She was a member of the Church of The Nazarene and they had one of their churches in Queensbury.

Having a good friend like Barbara helped me a lot when our old neighbours began to give up their flats. When we'd first moved into our flat, the upstairs neighbours were really nice and we'd got on really well with them, but the ones that moved in when they moved out were just the opposite. I can't remember what it was for, but one day one of our new upstairs neighbours came down to our flat. When he saw how nice we'd made it they wanted it for themselves and from then on they never stopped trying to drive us out.

The first thing they tried was flooding out my kitchen, and they kept on until one day when I was in the kitchen the ceiling fell down right on top of my back. The Council couldn't find a leak because there never was one, which meant they never stopped our upstairs neighbours from flooding us out. There was always water on my kitchen walls and in the end I was scared to go there just in case the ceiling fell down on top of me again.

When flooding me out of the kitchen didn't work, they started flooding out the bathroom. When that didn't work they turned up their music so loud it rattled everything in my units and then my youngest son Philip went up to their flat and warned them to turn their music down or he'd sm⌐sh up their Stereo. But they still wouldn't turn it down so he went back up to their flat and smashed their Stereo to pieces, which didn't help because they just went and got themselves a new one.

Between the flooding, the noise and the stress I'd had with my cancer scare they drove me so close to a nervous breakdown that I had to get some help, and I managed to get some counselling at the Willows Medical Centre in Queensbury. My Counsellor's name was Marlene and she was the one who got me on courses for stress and then for depression. When Marlene was transferred to Parks Medical Centre on All

Saints Road off Great Horton Road, I carried on seeing her there.

Though Marlene did help me a lot, neither she nor the courses she got me on could stop the stress from getting worse when my son, Philip moved out to live with his girlfriend. As soon as they knew he wasn't living with me, they turned up the music so loud that when the District Nurse came round she was so shocked by the amount of noise they were making she went up and asked them to turn it down.

The District Nurse went away so annoyed by what they were putting me through that she phoned me up and gave me a number to ring. The number put me straight through to the head of all the Council housing, and after I'd told him what was going on he rang me back to tell me a Housing Association was building some sheltered housing on the Woodside Estate and asked me if I would consider moving to one of their new bungalows.

Of course I grabbed at the chance with both hands, and the one interview I had with a manager from the Housing Association was enough to get my name on their housing list. Then all I had to do was to wait for the builders to finish the bungalow, which took a lot longer than it should have done, because they went bankrupt and I ended up with four or five dates that were months and months apart.

While I was waiting for my new home, my eldest son's girlfriend was taking me for Physio sessions to strengthen up my stomach. My Physio sessions were at St Lukes Hospital and I can't remember why we were on our way home by way of Wibsey, but we were waiting at the bottom of Buttershaw Lane for a gap in the traffic on Halifax Road when a nurse came flying out of Buttershaw Lane Doctor's Surgery.

The nurse wasn't properly looking where she was going and she hit the back of our car so hard we were sent flying straight across Halifax Road. If she'd hit us only one second sooner we'd have been pushed right into the path of anything from 15 tons to 40 tons of articulated lorry. I must have been scared, but the funny thing is that while we were flying across Halifax Road in front of all that traffic, all I remember thinking is, 'at least I've got someone who will make me a headstone'.

Only the night before the crash I'd met a Monumental Mason in the Wheatsheaf pub at Queensbury, and he would have made me a really nice headstone- which I was lucky enough not to need. We went home without going to Casualty but as the day went on the pain in my neck, back and my stomach got so bad that when my eldest son came home from work he took us both to Casualty, where they gave me loads of X-Rays.

Some of X-rays were done on my back just to see if I'd damaged my spine - which it hadn't - but the force of the crash had given me hernias in my stomach just as it was healing nicely. Mr Griffith's understudy was supposed to repair the hernias but all he did was open me up, have a good look inside of my stomach, and he closed me up again without repairing them. So Mr Griffith had to open me up again and I had to go through two operations to repair the hernias instead of just the one, but at least I was still alive when I finally got a proper date to move into my new bungalow on the Woodside Estate.

Chapter Twenty

The name of the Monumental Mason I'd met the night before my crash at the bottom of Buttershaw Lane is Chris. He also had a flat in Queensbury and I had seen him now and again but the night before the crash was the first time we'd ever spoken. We'd got chatting in the Wheatsheaf, and after that night we always seemed to be bumping into each other though we probably shouldn't have met at all because by then I should have been in my new home on the Woodside Estate.

The first moving date I'd been given by the Housing Association was for September 2002, and I'd been all packed up and ready to move before I met up with Chris. But because the firm building the bungalows went bust, I was stuck with my nasty upstairs neighbours until the March of the following year. Having to spend another six months in Queensbury meant I saw a lot of Chris.

We seemed to get on really well together and what with him being so nice with me we got together at Christmas time. And now that I'm looking back on it all I think my big cancer scare must have put me into a really low point in my life, because I went and broke my own rules by letting Chris move into Woodside with me on St Patrick's Day 2003 (March 17th).

From the time I'd started my clubbing nights in Halifax, the rules I had for any man who wanted to be with me were really simple. I always told them right from the start, *"I like a drink. I like a smoke. I'm a bit greedy with everything. But I don't want to marry you. I don't want to get engaged, and I don't want you moving in with me. If I go out with you for a few years, I might get engaged to you just to show my commitment, but you won't be moving in with me."*

Not doing the same with Chris is why I've only got myself to blame for all the trouble I got from breaking my own rules, because even though Chris really behaved himself at first and we had a lot of fun with decorating the kitchen, once the kitchen was finished all he ever wanted to do was get drunk and watch the 'telly'. From then on 'badgering' him became the only way to get anything done, and even then he did nothing right.

If it was anything to do with decorating Chris would always come back with the wrong kind of paint, or the paint would be the wrong colour. I knew the only reason he did it was because he didn't want to do any work, or help me with the decorating and I can't say why I didn't just kick him out like I really should have done. But instead of helping myself I was too busy helping others through the Church of The Nazarene, which had made me their Secretary.

Even though I'd moved away from Queensbury, someone would always come to my new home to take me to the Church, and being their Secretary meant I got to see nearly everything that was sent to the Church, including some leaflets looking for people to train in Chaplaincy. When I thought of all the work so many people had put into me, I needed to give something back and Chaplaincy seemed perfect for me.

Any time I'm in a hospital I'm not laid in a bed or sat on a chair, just waiting for something to happen. The doctor's have their rounds to do and I have mine as well. Three times a day I'm off doing my rounds of all the Wards talking to all of the patients because I know from first hand how horrible and frightening it is when you're waiting for an operation.

Just because I laugh and joke my way through all my time in hospital, loads of people think that I'm not bothered by operations. Even the Anaesthetist I nearly always had told me he'd never known anyone else to come into the operating theatre laughing and joking as much me. But laughing and joking is just my defence against my own fear of operations. When it comes to the truth, I'm just as afraid as anyone else and that's why I've always used a laugh and a joke to help me get through it all.

Knowing how it feels to be waiting for an operation and having had so many myself, I'd realised I could help some of the other patients just by letting them know how brilliant the surgeons were and all they'd done for me. The way I talked to them always used to calm them down, and then they wouldn't be so frightened. That's why Chaplaincy seemed perfect for me and why I put myself down for the Course.

The Course taught us how to talk to people and what to do in different situations. We learned how to be with people from all sorts of different countries, cultures, and religions. We didn't have to learn their languages, but we did have to learn the proper approaches with polite sayings from their cultures, such as, "Hello!" How are you? Is there anything I can do for you?" and all that sort of thing.

As soon as I finished that part of the Counselling Course I went on to learn Bereavement Counselling, and once I'd passed every part of the Course I started working on the Wards. We were only supposed to do one Ward one day a week for a year, but I didn't feel that I could help enough patients and so I used to go in for two days a week. In the end I was working on six of the Wards, which I'd been doing for quite a while when I started having my own problems with health.

When I was well enough to go back to the work, there were two Church of England people and a Catholic priest in the office. Instead of just giving me my hours, my pass and my luncheon vouchers, one of the Church of England people told me that 'they couldn't have me doing the work with all the time I was having off'.

The Catholic Priest sounded as shocked as I felt when he told them both- "I don't know how you can say that to Iris! She does more work than the rest of them put together!" Though I was grateful to the Catholic Priest for saying those things for me, it wasn't enough to get over the shock and when I left that office I never went back.

I'd put my heart and soul into the Chaplaincy work, but I suppose that I was the one that really needed some Chaplaincy done for me because Chris had given up any attempt at working, and all he ever wanted to do was drink Cider from morning to night while 'vegetating' in front of the 'telly'.

Nothing I did or said to Chris could ever get past his drinking. There were loads of times that I did kick him out along with all the times he left on his own, like after the time he lost his temper and tried to choke me. But I was too bloody soft with him and it was still going on like that in the early part of 2005 when I went to a Charity 'Do' for the Boxing Day 2004 Tsunami survivors.

Our Community Association went by the name of Royds and they'd raised over £30 million (GBP) to regenerate the three Estates I'd lived on at one time or another. As part of their regeneration, Royds built some new Community Centres. One of the new Centres was just across the road from where I lived, and Royds were letting a group of Beauticians and Therapists use it to hold a Tsunami Appeal 'Pamper' Day.

There weren't many girls I knew of on the Estates that had the sort of money to spend on beauty parlours, massages, manicures, pedicures, facials and all the sort of things that better off women take for granted as an important part of their lives. So when the leaflets advertising the event went up in the Centre, all the girls were getting excited and I heard them talking about it. And when the day finally came there were loads of people at the event including a Police Community Building Team. The policewomen on the team weren't shy when it came to getting some 'pampering', and neither was I.

Treatments like Massage, Reflexology and Reiki were all being done in the small rooms outside the main hall. Like I said in my rules for men- 'I'm greedy with everything' and I'd treated myself to Massage, Reflexology and Reiki before I went off to the main hall for my Hot Wax Hand Massage, Manicure, Pedicure and Foot Spa, after which I was planning on getting my face painted like a Tiger.

While I was making my way to the main hall I heard some of the girls talking about how nice their Indian Head Massage had been. Up to then, as far as I remember, I wasn't really thinking about having an Indian Head Massage because of all the lumps and bumps I had in my head from all the holes they'd drilled and filled in my skull when Mr Towns had clipped my aneurysm.

I was all right with my hairdresser who I'd known for loads of years, but I wasn't sure how a therapist I'd never met would feel about having to work on a head full of lumps and bumps. I suppose I was much too self-conscious to even ask for a head massage until I was having my Foot Spa right next to where the therapist was working.

Just sitting there with my feet in the Spa watching everyone else being made so relaxed from their head massage made me start wanting one for myself. Then when I saw how the policewomen couldn't wait to take off their equipment belts and their Stab Vests I thought, "why shouldn't I have one too?"

Just after my foot Spa ended, the therapist finished doing the last policewoman's head massage, and as soon as she'd gone I went and told the therapist about the lumps and bumps on my head thinking he wouldn't want to do a head massage on me.

When I'd finished explaining why there were loads of lumps and bumps in my head he just smiled and told me that everyone had these on their heads. The only thing that would worry him was if he had to work on someone with a head as smooth as an egg. And of course I could have an Indian Head Massage if that was what I wanted.

I now know there are loads of different head massages that all call themselves an Indian Head Massage, but this was the real thing from India and it was so nice it's hard to explain how it feels when all of the tension comes out of your head, your shoulders and your back.

Women who've had their hair in really tight curlers will know how it's such a relief when they're taken out, and the feeling you get from a real Indian Head Massage is something like that, only better. It's like all the stress and tension comes out the top of your head, and I loved it.

Having the Indian Head Massage made it too late

to get my face painted like a Tiger, but I didn't mind because I'd never felt so relaxed in my life and it was really worth it when the therapist came and talked to me after the 'do' was over.

Now before I go on, I have to tell you that my therapist says this is 'my' story, and all I'm allowed to put down about him is that he was so convinced that everyone's brain has the power to recover from stroke that he'd spent nearly six years training in different Complementary Therapies.

He'd also thought there was something 'extra' that would add a lot more to helping people recover from stroke, even after many years of being disabled and he thought he'd found it. What was even more interesting to me was that the therapist was one of the Directors of Royds Community Association, and he told me he was setting up a Complementary Therapy Clinic which would be held every Sunday at our Woodside Centre, and it was going be free to all the residents of Royds.

He said most of his therapies would be available to all the residents who wanted to try them, but as he was still studying his new therapy he could only take me on as a Case Study. He'd done this with Paul Knowles, one of the founders and Treasurer of the South West Bradford Stroke Support Group who was responding well.

I would have said yes straight away, but before I could the therapist made me the same promise he'd made to Paul Knowles. First he made it very clear that he didn't know if he could help me at all, but he was willing to try, and wouldn't treat me like a 'Guinea Pig' if I wanted to be a Case Study for him.

He also said that when my time as his Case Study was over he would keep on treating me for free as long as we were getting improvements, or until I wanted to stop. That was nearly six years ago, and he's stuck to his word through a whole load of illness and accidents, which is all he's going to let me say. And now I'm going to move on to my first Complementary therapy treatment, which was quite a while after I'd first met the therapist, and by then some of my health problems had got a lot worse.

Three days before I went for my first treatment I'd woken up knowing I'd had a mini stroke (TIA) during the night, and I must have looked really ill when I went in for my treatment because the therapist made me tell him why I looked so poorly. When he found out I'd had a TIA without getting a medical check-up, he was so concerned that he wasn't even going to take my notes (medical history) until I told him I wouldn't see a doctor unless I had my treatment.

When I'd gone in for that first treatment, fifteen years had already passed since my aneurysm had burst and I was still blind in my left eye. The black wall still ran out from the centre of my nose and I still had tunnel vision in my right eye. The left side of my mouth was really drooped, and ever since my tumour operation my left arm had been spastified across my chest. My left wrist was bent into what they call a 'Swan's neck' and the left hand fingers were digging so hard and painful into the palm of my hand I had a right battle to put on my brace.

Over the years I'd used my right arm so much it was giving me serious problems. Every now and again it would just let go of what it was carrying, and I'd been told the only way to fix my right arm was with an operation. I dreaded this because I didn't know how I would cope without the use of both hands.

A lot of my left leg muscles looked all wasted away, and no one had managed to get my left leg to bend at the knee in all the time since my aneurysm. So I'd had to learn a different way of walking, which was always slow, and because I'd recently broken a bone in my foot my walking was even slower when I went in to have my first treatment.

My left foot had such painful hammer toes that the first toe kept me awake at night and it had to be straightened with an operation. There was no sensation in lots of places around my body, including my left hand, buttocks and waist. Between my stomach operations and the car crash I was having bladder and bowel incontinence.

The muscle cramps and spasms I was constantly getting in my neck, leg and jaw were so painful there were times I would have cried if I could (crying had become really hard for me after I'd had the aneurysm). The spasms in my jaw were so severe I was forced to wear a gum shield at night to stop me from harming my teeth. I still had bouts of Asthma, and I was so tired of fighting illness all the time I was on Prozac for depression as well as tablets for blood pressure, a muscle relaxant and painkillers, along with tablets for heartburn and nausea.

There was no fun in my life any more because I was always so tired I slept for most of the time, and when I was awake I couldn't eat. If I tried to eat even half of a sandwich I would just vomit it up, and I can't tell you how horrible my heartburn was even though I was on tablets for it.

Without being able to have some fun in my life, I'd finally reached the end. I was so tired of fighting non-stop illness that I'd made up my mind I'd have no more treatments and no more operations. But this was another avenue to any I'd tried before, and I was going to give it a go no matter what the therapist said.

When I make up my mind that's all there is to it, so the therapist never stood a chance of making me go away by just taking my notes. He could tell I wasn't pretending when he'd finished taking my notes and I'd told him again that I wasn't going to have any more treatments of any kind if it wasn't the treatment I'd come for. I kept insisting I wouldn't see a doctor until he'd given me the treatment and in the end I persuaded him to agree with me on the condition that I had to tell him how I felt all the time. And if there were any reactions he didn't like, then he would stop my treatment straight away.

That first treatment was so weird because I had it fully dressed and the therapist didn't do very much. All he did was a few little moves with his fingers and thumbs on different parts of my body, and then he'd leave the room for a while. All the movements were really light and he didn't seem to be doing much, but strange things were happening to my body.

While he was doing the very first little move with his fingers and thumbs in the small of my back, a sharp pain shot from where he'd done the move and went right into my left lung. Then all of a sudden I went freezing cold, but only down my left side followed by my buttocks going a funny sort of numb.

A while later my left arm got pins and needles along with a strange, light throb or pulse in the palm of my left hand. And at one point the therapist almost stopped the treatment when I told him I felt something like I did when I woke up from having the mini stroke. But after I told him it felt nice in a funny way I couldn't explain, he agreed to keep going.

During the two days after my treatment I did have some pain in my hips, buttocks and lungs but the pain kept fading away and by the morning of the third day it had gone. But what surprised me the most was that by the time I'd had the second treatment, my left arm and left leg felt warm for the first time since my aneurysm had burst.

The left arm felt looser than it had since my tumour operation, and although I couldn't explain it I didn't feel as down as I did before I had my first treatment. By the time I'd had six treatments, the black wall stretching out from the middle of my nose had gone and I was just beginning to see out of my left eye for the first time in fifteen years.

My mouth had straightened up again. I'd stopped needing to wear a gum shield at night. My left arm was hanging loose by my side. My fingers were loosening up, I could move my thumb again, and once Mr Bollen had straightened out my hammer toe there was no pain to stop me from going to sleep at night.

The best news of all was that by the time I got to my ninth treatment my left knee was bending so well that I could sit cross-legged on the floor, and I managed to walk to the supermarket and back as well as walking all the way round the store. And the most important thing of all was that my positive attitude came back.

Being able to bend my knee, use my arm, and see again have all stayed with me. But so much has happened to me since I had my very first Complementary therapy session that my treatments became more about keeping me going than they were about getting me back to where I was before I had my aneurysm, because for every step the treatments helped me forward there was always something to pull me back.

Over the past six years my therapist has helped me recover from broken ribs and the whiplash I got from Chris pulling out in front of a speeding car. There were bowel, hernia and bladder operations with Mr Griffith the Colorectal Surgery Specialist, and Mr Flannagan the Urological Surgeon.

Mr Bollen gave me an operation to remove one of screws from my ankle to give it more mobility. He also gave me another operation to straighten out my hammer toe by putting a pin in it, and this is where I want to thank them all once again for all the help they've always given me.

Along the way my therapist has had to help me get through asthma, pleurisy, migraine, operations and depression, but the biggest, hardest and longest problems he's had to help me through are the problems that came from the horrible side effects of a prescription drug that couldn't and wouldn't get on with my body.

Before I leave this part of my story, my therapist needs me to let you know that I played a big part in all my improvements. Everything he helped me achieve was worked on by me until it got better and better. When my arm went loose by my side again, I stretched and moved it all the time, sometimes through a lot of pain until I could put my arm behind my back with no help from my right hand. And you should have seen the therapist's face when he found out I'd managed to carry a hot cup of coffee from the kitchen to my living room using my left hand.

When my leg bent at the knee for the first time in fifteen years I had really painful hammer toes but I never stopped walking and bending my knee, even when the effort of trying to walk kept affecting how well I could see out of my left eye, when I'd only just got my sight back again, which got better and better as the effort got less and less. So if you're looking for a road out of stroke disability you have to put in your share of the work.

Chapter Twenty-One

My only reason for letting Chris keep on living with me for so long was that my eldest son Mark had been trying to break us up, and I'd been digging my heels in because of the way he'd made me break up with Michael. In the end that wasn't enough to keep on living with someone that only wanted to argue and vegetate in front of the telly drinking Cider from morning to night.

Once I'd got Chris out of my life, my old self began to come back. For a long time one of the things I'd wanted to do was finish off my decorating, so I'd cleared out my main bedroom for painting and papering and that's why I was sleeping in my spare room on the night I got home late from having a laugh and a joke with Keith, my friend who lived across the Court.

It was close to midnight when I'd got home and all I'd wanted was to go to bed. While I'd been getting changed I'd suddenly needed the toilet, and what I'd forgot in my dash to the bathroom was that I'd told my son-in-law to leave his tools on the floor beside the spare bedroom door after he'd finished fitting a saucepan rack in my kitchen.

A broken bone in my foot had only recently healed and when I'd stepped on the tools it hurt so much it made me jump and lose my balance. My top half landed in the living room and my legs stayed in the hall with my left leg pointing down the hallway at a right angle to my body. The night was freezing cold and I was stuck where I was in horrible pain.

My dog Buster must have known there was something seriously wrong because he came and lay down tight beside me and stayed all through the night, from somewhere round midnight to eight in the morning, which probably saved me from serious hypothermia.

Though Buster did his best for me there was nothing he could do to help me with the pain which got so bad it made me vomit and lose control of my bowels. So thank God I'd asked Keith to give me a call in the morning when he went to get his daily paper, or I could have been laid there until I died of pain, cold, hunger or any combination of all three.

It was one of the longest nights of my life, and when Keith knocked on my door in the morning he heard me shouting. He got the ambulance out to me, but I'd locked the door when I'd got home and the paramedics had to go to my Housing Association, which gave them the wrong keys for my house, and it turned out lucky for me that I'd left one of my living room windows slightly open.

The paramedics forced the living room window open wide enough for one of them to climb inside, and then she opened the door for the other paramedic. One of them gave me some injections that didn't get rid of all the pain, but they were strong enough to keep me from passing out when they straightened my leg, put me on the stretcher, and then took me to Casualty.

After they'd assessed me in Casualty they took me off to theatre where an Anaesthetist put me out before they took me in to fix my broken hip. That's why I never got to see or talk to the surgeon before the operation, so I never got to find out how good the surgeon was.

The next thing I knew was waking up to find my family round my bed. What I couldn't work out when I first came round was why Chris was there with them. It wasn't until later on that I found out my daughter had rung Chris up when she'd heard I'd broken my hip, and then she'd brought him in with her which is how we ended up back together again.

All the while my hip was healing Chris was really helpful to me. He stopped drinking as much as he did before I'd made him go, which made me think he might have finally changed his ways. So I let him stay with me, and he was still behaving himself when I was ready to walk with a crutch.

That's when my hip began to hurt me really bad, and at first I thought the extra pain was from me getting used to standing and walking again. But the first time my therapist saw me walk he noticed my left foot wouldn't go flat on the floor. He could see that when I tried to walk I had to stand on the tips of my left toes, and when my therapist checked my pelvis it was that far out of line the sole of my left foot didn't even reach the top of my right ankle.

My therapist could have levelled my legs by straightening out my pelvis, and he could have done it right away but he wouldn't until I'd seen Mr Bollen. He said that was because he couldn't see inside my leg, and that meant he had no way of telling how well the break had healed, or how the surgeon had plated the break.

When I did as my therapist said and saw Mr Bollen, he gave us the go-ahead and my therapist carefully levelled my pelvis over several treatments until there was only about an eighth of an inch between the lengths of both my legs.

Levelling my pelvis helped me a lot with my walking but it didn't get rid of the pain in my hip. So I had to go back to Mr Bollen who told me that he didn't do hips, but he could refer me to someone that did.

The 'someone' Mr Bollen referred me to is an Orthopaedic Surgeon whose name is Mr Veysi. Whatever he saw on the X-Rays made him recommend a total hip replacement without which he said I could end up with a 'floating hip', which would put me in a wheelchair for the rest of my life.

I've said before that I've learned to know what a surgeon is really like just by talking to them, and I knew that if anyone was going to save my walking it would be Mr Veysi who was kind enough to book me in for a total hip replacement.

I was all set for my total hip replacement and there was only one more day to go when poor Buster suddenly died. A few days before he died, Buster was bouncing around when I let him out for his morning toilet.

By the time it got to Buster's evening toilet his back legs had gone so bad we had to carry him into the garden, and though we did get some pills from the Vet they didn't help poor Buster who died a few days after we started him on the pills.

Anyone who's ever owned and loved a dog like I have will know that Buster's death was like losing a family member, and if it wasn't for Keith I don't know how I could have coped or what I would have done about Buster's ashes.

I'd quickly arranged two funeral services for Buster before I went in but I wouldn't have been able to get his ashes if it wasn't for Keith who took them and kept them safe for me. So I'm taking this chance to thank Keith for all he's done for me and all he did for my dear Buster.

Keith taking care of Buster ashes for me meant I was able to go-ahead with the operation, and Mr Veysi is such a good surgeon that the morning after my hip replacement I got out of bed and walked with no problem.

Later on that very same day, they came to take me down for an X-Ray and when they lifted me onto the trolley my side got banged so hard it put my new hip out, sending me into horrible pain.

With my new hip being my last chance of not having to spend the rest of my life in a wheelchair, Mr Veysi held a conference on how they were going to fix it. I think it was during the conference that Mr Veysi got the idea of a much longer plate.

The new plate Mr Veysi designed went nearly all the way from my hip to my knee, and after the second operation I was back to walking with a Zimmer Frame. But I don't know what was going on between my luck, my hip and me, because it wasn't long before I was back in agony.

All I'd wanted to do was to go to the toilet, but when I went in I couldn't use it because of a big disability frame that was sitting over the toilet. The frame was made for a much bigger person than me and someone must have forgot it was there. I was in such a hurry to 'go' I tried to move the frame by myself and the frame was so heavy my hip popped out, which made me scream with pain.

The nurses at the nearby 'Nurses Station' came running into the toilet where they found me just propped against my Zimmer unable to move at all, and after they managed to put me in bed I could have died from the pain which I had to put up with far too long.

Because of my stroke, Mr Veysi didn't want to put me through yet another operation, so a couple of times they took me to Theatre where they tried pushing the hip into place without Mr Veysi being there. When that didn't work, they put me in bed with weights attached to my leg. But this only gave me more pain and in the end they took me back to Theatre and this time Mr

Veysi was there.

He put my hip back into its proper place and then there was no more pain when I woke up back on the Ward. Being without pain meant that at last I could have a proper laugh and a joke with the nurses looking after me as well as with the physios that came to work on the Orthopaedic Ward.

I don't think the physios that came onto the Ward to work with the patients had ever worked with someone like me, and they weren't too sure about what I could do or how much I could take. So I asked them what was needed to strengthen up my hip. Then I got them to give me another Zimmer Frame, which I used to make up my very own exercises.

Before I go on about my recovery I have to say it's no wonder Mr Bollen and Mr Veysi are such good friends, because both of them are such lovely men as well as being brilliant Surgeons. Every single day Mr Veysi comes in to see all his patients before its time for him to start work, and then he does the same every evening after he's finished his work. Even on Saturdays and Sundays Mr Veysi comes in to check up on his patients which he did on every day and weekend I spent in the BRI.

Now it's back to the exercises I'd made up, and they helped me so much that at first I thought I'd be able to go to my youngest son's wedding in Mexico. But the more I thought on the length of the flight the more I knew it was going to be much too long of a flight for me, and in the end I decided I'd have to miss out on the wedding. I didn't want to lose my deposit, so I went to the Travel Agents and switched my son's wedding in Mexico for a holiday in Portugal.

Chris was supposed to go to Portugal with me, but the better I'd got the further he'd slid back into his drinking and 'vegetating'. He never wanted to go anywhere decent with me, and at first he said he was having trouble with getting the money to pay for his passport which soon turned into him creating loads of arguments with me. After a while his arguing got so bad I had no choice but to make him leave.

Going to Portugal on my own wasn't what I really wanted, so I switched it for a cruise in Egypt where I'd always wanted to go. Soon after I'd booked I was having a chat with my old friend Kevin and I mentioned the cruise on the Nile. And just in case you don't remember Kevin, he was the taxi driver that took me to Halifax when I first started my clubbing nights, and he was the same Kevin I'd sat with in the taxi office after he'd begun to go blind.

Kevin needed to go to The Centre for the Blind. I needed to pay off some of the balance on the cruise and we arranged to meet up in the town. Up until then Kevin hadn't said much about me going to Egypt, but while we were at the Travel Agents he told me he'd always wanted to go there just as much as me. When he asked me if I'd mind if he came along, there was no reason for me to say no and I liked his company, so I agreed and right there and then he booked his place on the cruise.

Chapter Twenty-Two

While we were waiting to go to Egypt I'd wanted some Rose trees for my garden, and my eldest son Mark had taken me to the Garden Centre in our big DIY called B&Q (A UK chain of large Do It Yourself Stores). We were just looking around the Garden Centre when some plants caught my eye and I didn't notice that someone had spilled some gravel.

When I went for a closer look I slipped on the gravel and fell, hitting my head so hard I was nearly knocked unconscious. The only thing that kept me from passing out was my son shouting, "MUM! MUM! MUM!" Every time my son shouted "MUM!" it shocked me back to consciousness and that's how he kept me from going under.

He was shouting so loud that some of the staff came running over to see what was happening and he made them fetch me a chair along with a drink of water. The staff wanted to know if they needed to get me an ambulance, but I wouldn't go to Casualty because I'd banged my new hip when I fell.

Mr Veysi and Mr Bolland, or someone they would recommend are the only ones I was going to let anywhere near my new hip and the X-Rays Mr Veysi took showed I hadn't damaged it. When the Optician checked my eyes there was no sign of a bleed and that meant I'd somehow managed to get away with the fall, but I couldn't get away with anything when it came to dealing with Chris.

I was at the Opticians when he came round to my house with some flowers he'd bought for me. My eldest son's partner was in the house and she took them off him for me. That should have been the end of it, but Chris must have been hoping a bunch of flowers would be enough to get us together again, and when his plan didn't work he started phoning me night and day.

The weird thing was that every time Chris phoned me up he could tell me what I'd been doing, as well as the names of everyone that had been to visit me. He knew so much about me it was obvious there was someone watching the house, and I would have been driven into a nervous breakdown if someone I knew hadn't seen Chris lurking in one of the empty bungalows about fifty yards from my house.

He'd been watching me from there, and after I got the police involved Chris was forced to leave his hiding place. But he still wouldn't stop phoning me up, and he still wouldn't leave me alone. We kept seeing him walking past my house or wandering very close to it and then someone tried to break into my home. I can't prove it was Chris, but whomever it was tried to kick their way through my back door.

When that didn't work they tried to force my windows open. At three different times, three different windows got damaged so bad by someone trying to force them open they all had to be replaced by my Housing Association. But they wouldn't change the standard locks on my doors for high security ones, so my son had to change them for me. And that was the way I had to live until it was time for my cruise on the Nile which finally got me some peace from Chris and his stalking.

Our flight took us to Luxor, and from there we went by Coach to the ship where I got a proposal of marriage on my very first night aboard. All I'd done was walk across the dance floor to the bar near to where a handsome young Egyptian stood. I wasn't at the bar for more than a moment or two before he came over and started 'chatting me up' which I didn't mind at all.

He turned out to be the camera and video man working for the cruise ship, and before I knew where I was he'd asked me to marry him. I might not have been joking when I told him that if we got married I could work with him on the cruise ships, to which he replied that 'when' we got married he didn't want me working. He would look after me, and then I could stop at home and have his babies for him- which would have been bloody clever of me at fifty-eight with a hysterectomy!

Though it did me the world of good to get a proposal from such a handsome man, there was no chance of me getting married to him or anyone else, which was no reason for me to turn down a bit of romance in my life. Throughout the cruise we had plenty of 'snogging sessions' but that was as far as I was ever going to let it go, though I do have say that those sessions were some of the highlights of the cruise.

Apart from that, the biggest highlight of the cruise came when we went to see the Valley of the Kings. With some help from Kevin and a big, bald headed fun-loving man we'd met on the cruise, I got to look at everything I'd ever dreamt of. The only problem was that I put so much effort into the Valley of the Kings that I never got to see the Valley of the Queens.

By the time the coach got us to the Valley of the Queens my hip was aching so much that I stayed by the coach while the others went off. I wasn't there very long before a shopkeeper came over to tell me not to stand in the sun, and then he invited me into his shop. I wasn't sure it was safe but when I looked at our driver he returned my look with one that told me I'd be all right, and then I followed the man into his shop.

The first thing he did in the shop was to give me a drink that was nice and cold. When he told me to help myself to snacks, I tried telling him that I had no money on me and that I couldn't pay him. But every time I talked about money he said he didn't want any money from me. Then he went and got me a gift, which I didn't feel I could take without paying him something for it. And once again he told me that he didn't want money from me. He said he just wanted to give me a gift.

That shopkeeper was really nice with me and while

we were talking he told me he had a brother who lived in London, which gave us a lot to talk about until the others came back. As I was walking out of the shop to join up with the others, he put a shawl across my shoulders as another gift to me even though he knew I would never be back his way.

I can't speak for anyone else when I say that all Egyptians I met on the cruise were some of the nicest people you could ever meet. They couldn't seem to do enough for you, and I won't pretend I wasn't flattered when the crew started calling me the 'Golden Queen'.

I'd had my hair dyed blonde for a while and my natural colour was showing through. There was something about my aneurysm that lightened my hair from its naturally deep auburn to a sort of copper colour that gleamed under the Egyptian sun, and that's why the Egyptian crew began calling me the 'Golden Queen'.

Everything about the crew and the way they organised the cruise was brilliant. They even had an 'Egyptian Night' where we got to eat Egyptian food and dress in Egyptian clothes. At first I was nervous when I heard we were going to be served with Egyptian food because of all the things I'd been told about the way they ate sheep's eyeballs, and how I'd be insulting them if I refused to eat one when it was offered to me. But I needn't have worried about sheep's eyeballs because there were no eyeballs at all and their food is beautiful.

It wasn't only the Egyptians I met and the crew on the ship who were brilliant with me. All the other passengers were really friendly and they were always ready for a chat, a laugh and a joke. Some of them gave me their names and telephone numbers for us to keep in touch.

At the end of the cruise, loads of them were cheering me on while we were waiting for our coaches. Some of them even came up to me just to tell me what an inspiration they thought I was and how they'd never ever forget me, which I didn't really deserve because I was only doing what I had to do to make the most of my trip to Egypt.

There are only two regrets I have about the time I went to Egypt. The first is that no one told us about the extra week we could have had in Sharm el Sheikh for only £50.00 (GBP), until it was far too late. The second regret is that almost as soon as I got home Chris started with the phone calls all over again, and though this time he never spoke a single word I always knew it was Chris from the 'hiss' of his Cider bottle.

That was a big mistake on his part if he wanted to get back with me because the background 'hiss' of his Cider bottle reminded me of his drinking and vegetating. I called the police who gave him a final warning and although he didn't completely stop, things had settled down enough for me to go away for a short break in Scarborough with my eldest son's partner.

It was during our break in Scarborough that my legs started hurting so bad there were times I couldn't walk. After I got home from Scarborough my therapist did all he could to get rid of the pain, but whatever he did would only last for a couple of days at the most and over the next few months all the improvements we'd fought so hard to get began to slip faster and faster away from me.

Going backwards like that took all the fun out of my life and I began to get really depressed. I felt dead tired all the time, but when I went to bed I couldn't sleep. Then I began to get horrible headaches that slowly got more and more often, and they got so severe that all I could do was get into bed and pray for them to go away.

I'd got to the point where I could only just cope when all of the horrible symptoms I'd had with my tumour returned, and I got scared the tumour was back. Nearly two months of hell went by with me getting worse with every day that passed. My therapist told me to go and see Mr Griffith, or at least talk to my doctor, but for the third time in my life I'd given up on hope and I don't know what would have happened to me if I hadn't left a box of one of my tablets on my coffee table on a day when my therapist came to treat me.

My therapist was curious enough to take a look at the name of the drug and then he asked me why it wasn't on the list of drugs I'd given him when I first started my treatments. I told him that at the time he'd put down the names of all my prescription drugs I hadn't been on it. Someone I'd never seen before had put me on it when my hip popped out in the BRI, and as far as I knew it was just another painkiller.

Not knowing why I'd been given the drug and not having told him I'd been put on it really surprised my therapist, who surprised me in turn by telling me it was really a muscle relaxant. Then he took out and read aloud the leaflet that came with the box and all the horrible symptoms I was getting were listed as possible side effects of the drug.

When he got home, my therapist took a much deeper look into the drug and what he found concerned him so much he made me make an urgent appointment with my doctor who immediately took me off the drug, and I was sent deep into the living hell of drug withdrawal.

Not every drug suits everyone who is put on it, and I also know that this one suited me so badly that from the time it tried to kill my legs in Scarborough until after my therapist found a way to help me out of withdrawal, it put me through such a living hell for about eighteen months that I can't bring myself to talk about it.

There might come a time when the memory of that living hell has faded, but that time isn't yet because I still get horrible headaches and other side effects that my therapist is having to help me through. But the most important thing of all is that I'm almost free of it now, and I've only got one more hernia operation.

In fact I'm feeling so much better now that after months of being stuck in my house with deep depression, pain, headaches, sleeplessness, muscle, bowel, bladder and stomach problems I recently went to see Gilbert O'Sullivan in Concert at St George's Hall in Bradford. I got to have a lovely long chat with Gilbert's sister before the show and then some lovely cuddles with kisses on my cheek from Gilbert and his brother at the 'signing' after the show.

I've also just come back from having a holiday in Bridlington where I made loads of new friends. I managed to get there and back all on my own by bus and apart from a woman who tried to 'chat me up' and sat too close to me while I was waiting for the bus on my way home I had such a brilliant time I can't wait to go on holiday again.

Right now I'm happy to say that the real Iris is finally coming back again, and she's ready for loads of fun and loads of laughter. And wherever your journey has taken you, I hope you'll be as lucky as me in the way that someone will always come forward to help, the same as there's always been someone to help me when I've needed it the most.

Note:
Gilbert O'Sullivan (born 1 December 1946) is an Irish-English singer-songwriter, best known for his early 1970s hits "Alone Again (Naturally)", "Clair" and "Get Down". The music magazine Record Mirror voted him the No. 1 UK male singer of 1972. Worldwide he has charted 16 top 40 discs; including six number one songs, the first of which was 1970's "Nothing Rhymed" His most successful recording period was between 1970 and 1980, though he has since recorded nine studio albums up to the 2011's (*Taken from Wikipedia*).

P.S.

I'm happy to be able to say that I'm almost free of the horrible adverse drug reaction that 'hit' me soon after I returned to England from the cruise, and now I'm back to having loads of fun.

I recently bought a white West Highland Terrier puppy that I've named 'Susie' and I'm looking forward to moving to 'Sheltered Housing', on the East Coast, close to where I had so many good times with my parents when I was growing up.

Just in case you haven't already guessed, or worked it out from his profile, my 'writing helper, my therapist, and my author are all one and the same person. And he still says this is my story, so you won't be hearing much more about him!

I hope my story inspires you when times are tough, and I wish you all the best....*Iris.*

Printed in Great Britain
by Amazon.co.uk, Ltd.,
Marston Gate.